World Record-Breakin
PREET CH

THE EXPLORER'S GUIDE TO GOING WILD

Illustrated by Aditi Kakade Beaufrand

wren &rook

To my niece, Simran, and nephews,
Karanveer and Arjan

First published in Great Britain in 2024 by Wren & Rook

Text copyright © PC Expeditions Ltd. 2024
Illustrations copyright © Aditi Kakade Beaufrand 2024
All rights reserved.

The right of Preet Chandi and Aditi Kakade Beaufrand to be identified as the author and illustrator respectively of this Work has been asserted by them in accordance with the Copyright, Designs & Patents Act 1988.

ISBN: 978 1 5263 6684 9

3 5 7 9 10 8 6 4

MIX
Paper | Supporting responsible forestry
FSC® C104740

Wren & Rook
An imprint of
Hachette Children's Group
Part of Hodder & Stoughton
Carmelite House
50 Victoria Embankment
London EC4Y 0DZ

An Hachette UK Company
www.hachette.co.uk
www.hachettechildrens.co.uk

Printed and bound in Great Britain by Clays Ltd, Elcograf S.p.A.

Contents

Introduction: No Adventure is Too Small — 4

Chapter One: The Good Explorer's Backpack — 9

Chapter Two: Navigating Your Way — 26

Chapter Three: Build Your Own Shelter — 40

Chapter Four: Fuelling Up for Fun! — 52

Chapter Five: Get Outdoors! — 64

Chapter Six: Super Survival Skills — 75

Chapter Seven: Embrace Mistakes — 89

Chapter Eight: The Best Adventures Are with Friends! — 99

Chapter Nine: Solo Exploration — 112

Chapter Ten: Where to Go on Your Next Adventure — 123

Chapter Eleven: Making Do with What You Have — 137

Chapter Twelve: Go Wild with Nature Crafts — 149

Chapter Thirteen: Night-Time Magic — 158

Chapter Fourteen: Embrace Your Inner Explorer — 169

Chapter Fifteen: The Amazing Nature Treasure Hunt — 177

The Grand Finale: Your Adventure Awaits! — 183

INTRODUCTION

NO ADVENTURE IS TOO SMALL

HELLO!

I'm Preet Chandi and I love to explore! When I'm not working as a physiotherapist for the British Army, I get to go on incredible adventures all around the world. That's right, I've been on exciting journeys to hot climates like India and Kenya, and to freezing continents like Antarctica.

People often think that because I am in the Army and have been on some big adventures, I probably started exploring quite young, but that's not true. The first time I went camping was with the Army, I was nineteen years old and I'll never forget the mix of emotions I felt – **nervousness, excitement** and **curiosity** all at the same time.

Camping with the Army was a complete shock to my system. It was a far cry from anything I had experienced before. The training and the challenges were completely new to me, and it felt like stepping into a whole new world. There were so many things I was trying that I had never done before – **camping, reading a map, testing my survival skills**.

I can vividly remember the uncertainty I felt as I embarked on this new and unfamiliar journey. But you know what? **I was also incredibly excited.** That excitement was like a spark in my heart, pushing me to embrace the unknown.

Feeling this way when trying something new is entirely normal. It's OK to be a little nervous, but it's also important to let your excitement and curiosity guide you. Sometimes, the most incredible adventures begin with that first step into the unknown. So if you ever find yourself facing a new experience, remember that it's an opportunity to **grow, learn** and **discover** your own incredible adventures.

Think of this book as your passport to a world of exciting adventures. Just like a good explorer's backpack (which you'll learn all about in chapter one), it's packed with all the knowledge and skills you need to have amazing adventures. We've got a treasure trove of chapters waiting for you, each filled with tales from my expeditions, guidance on how to have your own adventures and activities you can do at home to become a master explorer. You will discover all the essential tools to pack in your backpack, master the secrets of navigation, learn how to build a shelter and so much more!

And most importantly, I'll show you that adventures don't have to be great big expeditions **and you don't always need to go far from home to have an amazing experience.** One of my favourite adventures was in the UK when I took my niece, Simran, camping for the first time. We had the best adventure, and it was only in my mum's garden!

Camping at my mum's house was a perfect first adventure for Simran because if we needed anything from inside the house, it was easy to grab. But some of our family had concerns. They were worried Simran would be too scared to sleep outside in a tent or that she might get cold and not enjoy it. Of course, these fears came from the members of my family who had never been camping before, so I explained that there was nothing to worry about. If we were well prepared, then we'd be all snug in the tent.

And camping was a success! Simran eagerly helped me set up the tent by passing me tent poles, and we worked together to put down the roll mats and lay the sleeping bags. We brought extra blankets from inside the house to make sure it was super snug, and to make it extra special, we hung fairy lights. It was magical. Simran and I brought toys and books inside the tent and settled in for an epic sleepover. After a few hours, Simran fell asleep. I kept an eye on her, checking every now and then during the night to make sure she was comfortable. And guess what? When morning came, Simran didn't want to leave the tent; she wanted to stay 'for a bit longer'.

She absolutely loved her first camping experience, and I cherished the adventure we had together. She had so much fun trying something new, even if it was just in the garden. It reminded me that adventures are all around us; they're just waiting to be explored!

So now I've embarked on a new adventure – writing this book – to teach you, lovely reader, just how easy it is to have an adventure and what it takes to be a good explorer. It's time to go wild by learning about nature, trying new things and making brilliant memories. Does this sound fun? Then let's get started!

Explorer's top tip

First of all, always remember to ask a trusted adult before you go on any adventures outside of your home. It's likely they'll want to tag along with you too!

CHAPTER ONE

THE GOOD EXPLORER'S BACKPACK

Why we need to prepare for adventure

Going on an adventure is super exciting! The anticipation of going to a new place or trying something new always gets me jumping out of bed in the morning. But before you can go on your own adventure, you need to think about what problems or dangers you might come across. That's why it's important to always be prepared when you go exploring. We need to make sure we have the right equipment, know how to use it safely and have planned our adventure carefully.

If we don't, we might end up in real danger or else REALLY HUNGRY like I was in my ultra-marathon in Morocco.

My 156-mile race

I read a book called *100 Toughest Challenges* and learned about this incredible race in Morocco. It was a 156-mile race in the scorching desert and although it sounded hard, I was inspired to take part.

I had never run so far before, and the sun was going to be really hot. But the race was spread out over six days, so I didn't have to run it all at once. **We had to run a different distance each day and they gave us these small cards that said how many miles there were between the checkpoints. And you know what those checkpoints had? Water! That was important because I had to make my water last until I reached the next checkpoint.**

Running in the desert was challenging. The terrain varied from flat, compact sand to huge sand dunes that crumbled under my feet. The sand in some parts of the race was like a big soft pillow and my feet sank into it. To keep the sand out of my shoes, I had these cool things called 'gaiters' that went up to my shins. They helped me glide through the sand.

Even though I entered the race on my own, **I never felt alone.** There were people from all around the world doing the race, and everyone I met was awesome. I even shared a tent (tent 83) with other racers – eight of us in total – and we still keep in touch with each other today.

Making friends on that race was hugely important. On one scorching day, I had run out of water, and it was so, so hot. I had slowed down and was walking because it was so tough and I was so thirsty. The professional runners, who were really fast, started later than the rest of us, and a few of them ran past me. But then, one of them stopped. He saw me struggling, and he did something incredible. He linked his arm with mine and kept saying, 'allez, allez', which means 'go, go'. We jogged together to a nearby well. He got some water from the well and poured it over himself and I did the same. I felt so much better! I thanked him and he continued running. He was very quick! His encouragement got me through the hardest part of the challenge.

Luckily, I got to see him again at camp that night and could thank him properly. He had been so kind and helpful, even though helping me had slowed him down. It taught me that sometimes, no matter how much you prepare, unexpected things can happen. Like running out of water on a hot day. But if you're lucky, a kind stranger can help you get through the unexpected things and make a tough situation much better.

So if you ever come across a fellow adventurer who needs help, lend them a hand, because they'd do the same for you. **Teamwork and kindness can turn a challenging situation into a success story.** Together, you can take on any challenge that comes your way!

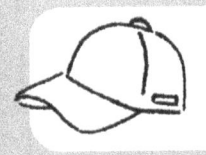

Desert marathon preparation

Packing the right supplies for this big adventure was essential. I needed a well-stocked backpack, and these items were key:

- **Trainers:** They had to fit properly and be comfortable.
- **Sun cream:** It was going to be very hot, and I didn't want to get burnt.
- **A cool hat:** To protect my face from the sun.

Can you guess what else I had to carry?

◯ Water and a lot of snacks!

My backpack is my trusty sidekick. I sometimes name the kit I carry with me. It makes me feel like I'm not alone on adventures. What would you call your backpack if you were doing a desert marathon?

I made a few mistakes when preparing for this race, but the biggest was not trying the food I had packed until I got there. I had bought some powdered milkshakes that looked tasty, but when I first tried them, tired and hungry at mile 13, I quickly discovered that they were disgusting! But I needed energy, so I had no choice but to drink the shakes.

By day four, I was more than halfway through the race. My legs were tired and achy, but I didn't give up. Some of the other food I had brought tasted better, so eating was easier, and it really helped to lift my spirits. I had brought freeze-dried mac and cheese with me and it was delicious! (Never heard of freeze-dried food? I'll tell you more about it on page 53!)

Finally, after six days, 156 miles, a few blisters and six packets of freeze-dried food, I crossed the finish line. What had started as a cool race I'd read about in a book had become a real-life adventure. I never thought I could do it, but I did. And when I finished, I started wondering about all the other cool things I might be able to do.

Adventures are like magical keys that unlock your potential. You've just got to start going on them.

How to prepare for adventures

Remember, even if things get tough, keep going. **Each step takes you closer to amazing places you never thought you could reach.** So get ready, future explorers – you've got a world of exciting challenges waiting for you!

Now it's time for you to prepare your explorer's backpack.

Create your own explorer's backpack

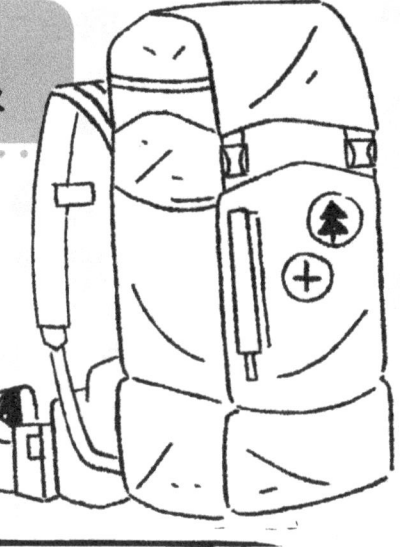

Let's make sure you have all the essentials you need for your own adventure. Find these items in your home and gather them up, then pack them in your trusty backpack.

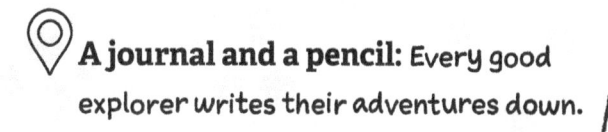

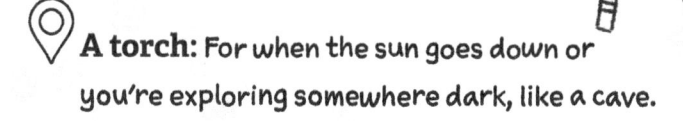

- **A journal and a pencil:** Every good explorer writes their adventures down.

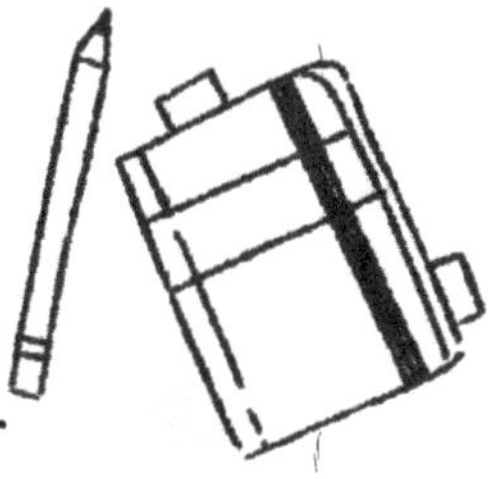

- **A torch:** For when the sun goes down or you're exploring somewhere dark, like a cave.

- **Snacks:** Keep your energy up with tasty treats. Fruit, a cereal bar or a packet of crisps will keep you going.

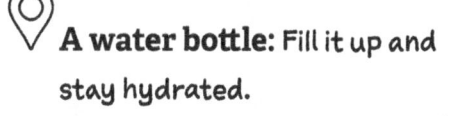

- **A water bottle:** Fill it up and stay hydrated.

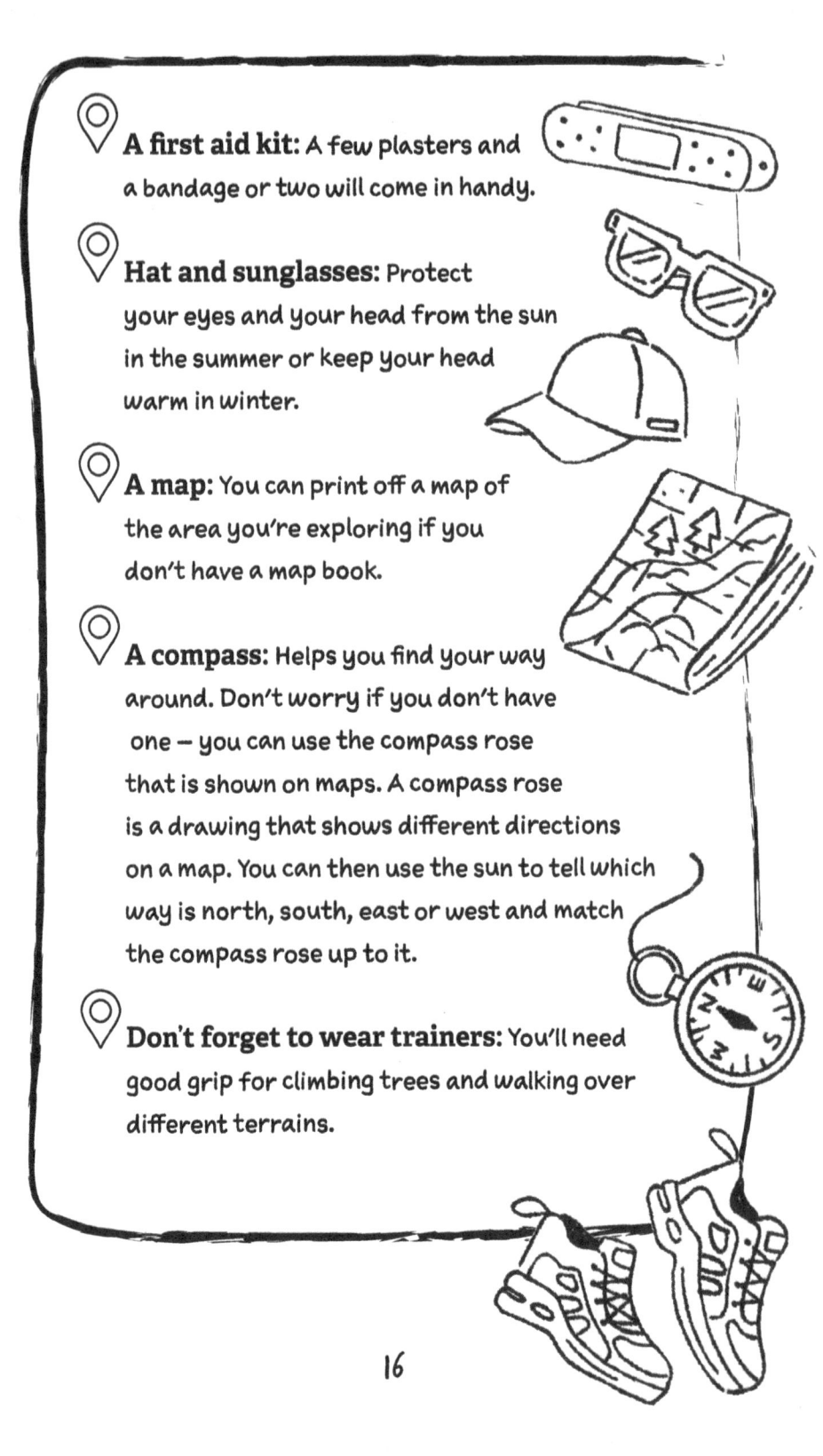

- **A first aid kit:** A few plasters and a bandage or two will come in handy.

- **Hat and sunglasses:** Protect your eyes and your head from the sun in the summer or keep your head warm in winter.

- **A map:** You can print off a map of the area you're exploring if you don't have a map book.

- **A compass:** Helps you find your way around. Don't worry if you don't have one – you can use the compass rose that is shown on maps. A compass rose is a drawing that shows different directions on a map. You can then use the sun to tell which way is north, south, east or west and match the compass rose up to it.

- **Don't forget to wear trainers:** You'll need good grip for climbing trees and walking over different terrains.

Explorer's top tip

Do you know what unexpected item every great explorer has in their backpack?

Toilet paper!

You never know when you might need it, so it's better to be prepared.

Now that we've looked at your essential explorer's backpack, let's think about what we'd add if we were going on a camping trip and how we'd pack it all up in the right order.

1. Start by placing your sleeping bag and spare clothes at the bottom — what comes out last goes in first. These are the things you'll use towards the end of the day when it's time to rest.

2. Having them at the bottom helps you to distribute the weight evenly and protect your back.

3. In the middle of your backpack, on top of the sleeping bag, add the heavier items for a comfortable load during your adventure.

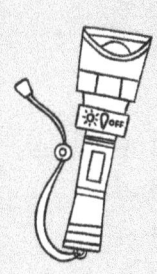

This includes your food, tent and cooking equipment. These are the things you'll need more often, so keep them easily accessible.

4. At the top, pack your quick-access items – snacks, hat, sunglasses, torch, first aid kit, map, compass and toilet paper. These are the essentials you want to reach quickly.

5. If your backpack has a side pocket, use it for your water bottle. This way, you can grab it easily whenever you're thirsty.

Now that your backpack is all set and you're brimming with excitement, let's look at how else we can prepare for our expedition. Adventures, whether big or small, are always better when you're well prepared.

Good preparation is your secret recipe for making sure your adventure is not just exciting but safe too.

Imagine you're about to explore a dense forest. You might find hidden waterfalls, fascinating wildlife and maybe even secret treasure (or at least that's what your imagination tells you). Now, what if it suddenly starts raining? Or you lose your way among the towering trees? **That's where preparation comes in handy.**

You need to think about the things you want to discover and the challenges you might face along the way. With a plan, you won't get lost and you'll know exactly what to do if it starts raining – bring out that trusty waterproof.

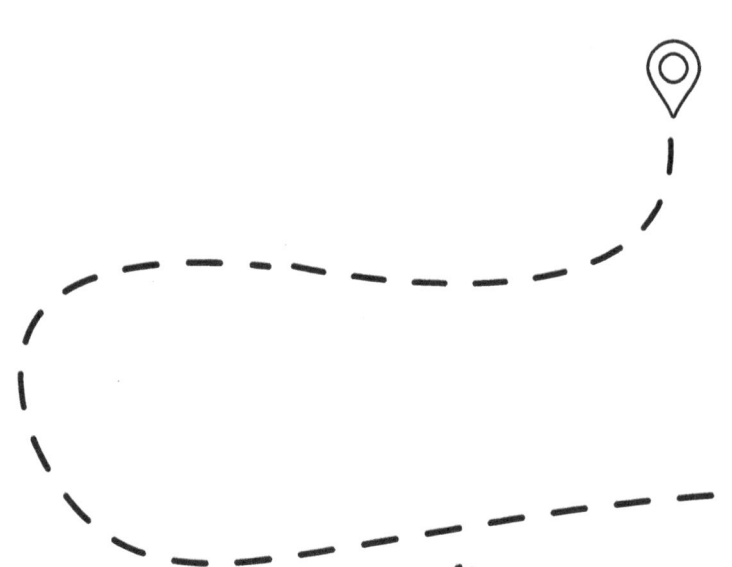

Adventure checklist

Adventure awaits, and to make sure it's a fantastic experience, you've got to take some time before you set off to plan like a pro.

Ask yourself:

What is the weather going to be like?
Is it going to be wet and muddy? Raincoat and wellies are a must. Or is it sunny and hot? Take sun cream and a sun hat instead.

How long will I be exploring?
Is it an all-day adventure? You'll need a backpack filled with snacks, water and a notebook to jot down your discoveries. But if you're planning an overnight camping trip, you'll also need a torch, a cosy sleeping bag and a tent for a good night's sleep.

Are there any special rules to follow at my destination?
Every adventure location can have its own set of rules and special things to know. If you're exploring a nature reserve, there might be

rules about staying on the marked trails to protect the plants and animals. Or if you're going to a historic site, there could be rules about not touching the ancient artifacts. Ask a grown-up to help you find out that information.

What equipment do I need? The list on page 15 is a great place to start.

Embrace the unknown

Here's a secret about adventures – **they often come with surprises!** Dealing with these surprises can be a bit tricky, like navigating through a forest trail you've never been on before. But adventures are all about having a positive attitude and being open to new experiences. You never know what amazing discoveries you might make or what exciting challenges you'll overcome.

The good explorer's quiz

Now, here's a fun challenge for you. Imagine you're a daring adventurer preparing to explore a mysterious island, and answer the questions below. You can use these questions to help you plan for any adventure.

Question 1: What should you bring to stay dry if it rains during your island adventure?
A) A sun hat
B) A waterproof
C) A swimsuit

Question 2: You're going to explore a dark cave on the island. What should you bring to help you see inside?
A) Sunglasses
B) A torch
C) A pillow

Question 3: Your adventure buddy got a small cut while exploring. What item from your explorer's backpack should you use to help them?
A) A notebook
B) A magnifying glass
C) A first aid kit

Question 4: You come across a sign that says, 'Do not feed the wildlife'. What should you do if you have some snacks with you?
A) Eat your snacks and leave the wrappers on the ground
B) Ignore the sign and feed the animals
C) Respect the sign and keep your snacks for yourself

Question 5: You discover a beautiful seashell on the beach. What's the best thing to do with it?
A) Leave it on the beach for others to enjoy
B) Take it with you as a keepsake
C) Bury it in the sand for safekeeping

How did you do? Find the answers on page 186.

Why not create your own adventure quiz? Think about what questions you'll need to ask yourself before planning your next expedition.

Adventure awaits!

You've thought about what you need for your adventure, you've packed your bag and now you're ready to go. Before you set off, remember my tips for being a fully prepared explorer:

📍 Preparation is the key to making your adventures go smoothly.

📍 Planning helps you know where you're going and what to do in case of surprises.

📍 Adventures can bring delightful surprises, so always stay curious.

And now, young adventurers, you're all set to become **true masters of exploration.** Your next thrilling adventure, whether in your local park or a far-off land, eagerly awaits. So gather your trusty explorer's backpack, unfurl your map and let the grand adventures commence!

CHAPTER TWO
NAVIGATING YOUR WAY

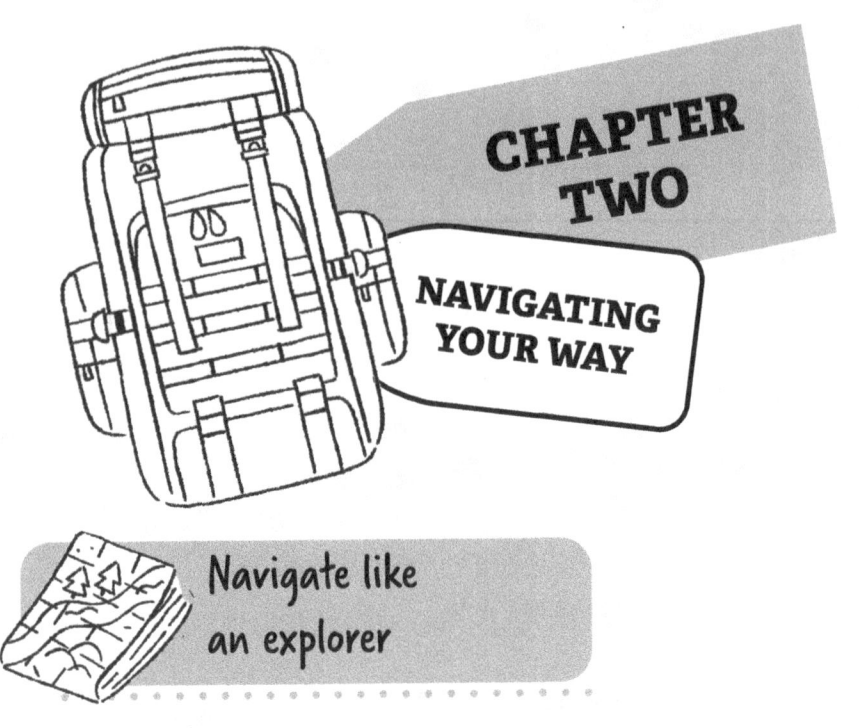

Navigate like an explorer

Are you ready to learn the secret art of finding your way, just like real adventurers do? Whether you're going to a local park, woods, forest or somewhere a bit further, knowing how to navigate is essential. Let's dive into the wonderful world of finding your way and get you all set for your exciting journey.

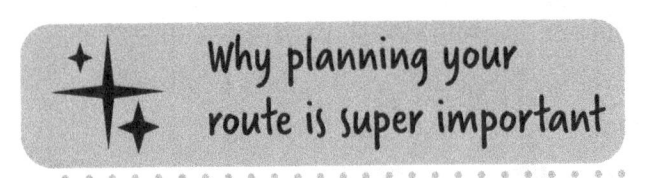

Why planning your route is super important

Even if you're going for a simple stroll in the park, planning your route is important. You need to know where you're going, how to get there and even when to cross the road safely. Imagine being in Antarctica, where it's a huge icy wonderland. You need tools like a GPS and a compass to navigate through the frozen wilderness.

Tools to help you find your way

Map-reading: Maps unlock the world. Learn to read them and you'll never get lost!

The stars: When the sun goes down, the stars become your friends. You can work out which way is north by finding the North Star. This is the brightest star in the Ursa Minor constellation. Find out more about this constellation on page 163.

A compass: A compass points you in the right direction.

The sun: If you're without a compass, the position of the sun can help you determine which way is north, east, south or west.

Plants: Moss tends to grow on north-facing trees and rocks in the northern hemisphere because they like the lack of sunlight, whereas trees and plants love the sunlight so tend to grow on the southern part of a hill.

Navigating the Antarctic wilderness: A compass, sun and GPS adventure

I've been to Antarctica on two adventures to see just how far I could go on my own. On each trip I had a special holder for my compass called a mount. I used this mount every day as it helped keep my compass in place so I could easily look at it and know which way I was going in the icy wilderness.

A compass is a small, round gadget with a special needle inside that points to the north and helps you figure out the other directions – east, west and south. Antarctica is a giant snow and ice landscape with no signs or posts on the way, and it's easy to turn in the wrong direction. My compass was my reliable guide, making sure I didn't go in circles.

However, I didn't want to strain my neck by staring at the compass all the time, so I used a clever trick – my shadow. When the sun was shining behind me, my shadow stretched out in front of me. As the sun moved across the sky during the day, my shadow would also move. I made sure to keep an eye on my shadow while also checking my compass from time to time to make sure I was still heading in the right direction. By using my shadow and my compass together, I was able to stay on track and navigate through the icy wilderness of Antarctica safely and confidently.

But sometimes, I faced challenging conditions known as 'whiteouts'. It's like walking inside of a marshmallow – I couldn't see anything in front of me. **When that happened, I couldn't use my shadow because it disappeared. On those days, I had to depend on my compass. When I didn't want to stare at my compass, I would concentrate on the tips of my skis and my ski poles. My compass helped me stay on the right path even when everything around me was white and hard to see.**

And every evening, I had another helpful gadget: my GPS. It gave me my exact coordinates, telling me precisely where I was. So between my compass, the sun and my trusty GPS, I managed to find my way around that snowy wilderness!

Sundial

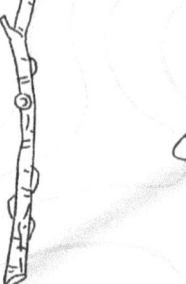

All right, let's make a sundial with just a stick! Follow these steps:

1. Find a straight stick. It could be about as tall as your arm.

2. Push one end of the stick into the ground so that it stands up straight. Make sure it's in a sunny spot.

3. Look at the shadow the stick makes on the ground.

4. Now, mark the tip of the shadow with a little stone.

5. Check back every hour and add a new stone to the tip of the shadow. You'll notice it's moved.

Do this for as many hours as you can and you'll have a stone marking each hour.

Have you noticed that the shadow is changing length?

In the morning, the shadow will be long. As the day goes on, it gets shorter.

Midday is when the shadow is the shortest.

In the afternoon, the shadow gets longer again until the sun sets and it becomes night-time.

And there you go! You've made a sundial. Now you can tell the time just by looking at where the shadow falls on the ground. You have your own clock powered by the sun!

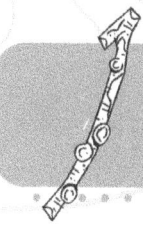

Sunny discoveries: Exploring shadows, seasons and Earth's spin

Earth's spin: Our Earth is like a big spinning top, turning around and around. That's what makes the sun appear to move across the sky during the day.

The sun's journey: The sun starts in the morning on one side of the sky (the east), and as the day goes on, it moves to the other side (the west). This makes the shadow from your stick change direction.

Seasons change: The shadow also changes as the

seasons do. In summer, the shadow might be shorter, and in winter it could be longer. That's because of how the Earth tilts and goes around the sun.

So by watching your stick's shadow, you can learn about the Earth and the sun, and even tell the time! It's like a cool science game you can play outside. Enjoy your shadow adventures!

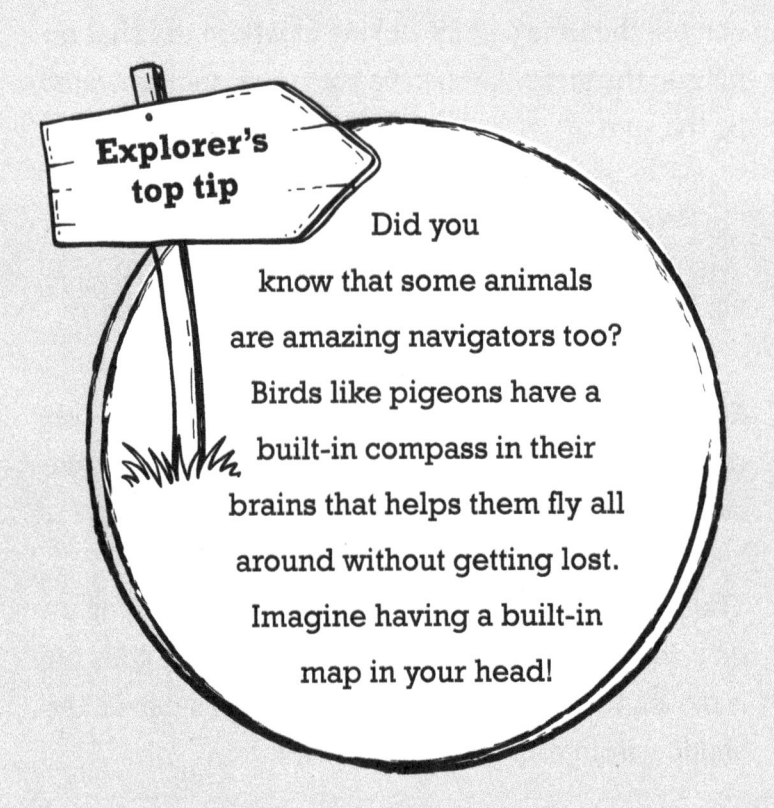

Explorer's top tip

Did you know that some animals are amazing navigators too? Birds like pigeons have a built-in compass in their brains that helps them fly all around without getting lost. Imagine having a built-in map in your head!

Overcoming obstacles and planning alternatives

Adventures aren't always smooth sailing. Sometimes, a road might be blocked or things might not go as planned. When this happens, you'll probably feel frustrated, but it just means your journey is going in a new direction. And guess what? It could be even better than the previous way you were heading!

Map-reading

Let's dig deeper into the wonderful world of navigation. Learning to read maps is an exciting skill that every adventurer should master.

A map is a diagram of an area of sea or land with all the roads, paths and terrains marked on it. To read a map, follow these steps:

1. Look at the title to know what the map is showing. For example, it could be a map of a zoo.

2. Find the compass rose. It looks like a star with N, S, E and W written on it. These letters stand for north, south, east and west. If you know which way is north (use a compass to figure this out), you can work out the other directions.

3. Use the legend/key to understand what the symbols on the map mean. It uses symbols or colours to show what things are on the map. For example, a little tree symbol might mean a forest, and a blue line might be a river. Check the key to understand the map better.

4. The scale tells you how big or small things are compared to real life. The scale is a line with numbers, often on the side of the map. If the scale says 1 inch equals 1 mile, and your destination is 2 inches away on the map, it means it's 2 miles away in real life.

5. Follow the roads, paths or symbols on the map to find your way to where you want to go.

Exploring world maps

Here's a challenge for you. Use the world map on the next page to find the places below and on page 38. Can you find the country you live in along the way?

1. The vast, frozen continent at the bottom of the map

2. A country in Africa known for its ancient pyramids

3. A country in Asia known for its great wall

4. The smallest continent in the world and the home of kangaroos

5. A country in Europe that is famous for the Eiffel Tower and croissants

6. A country that is known for stunning natural landscapes and also for maple syrup

7. A country that is famous for its vibrant carnival celebrations

North America

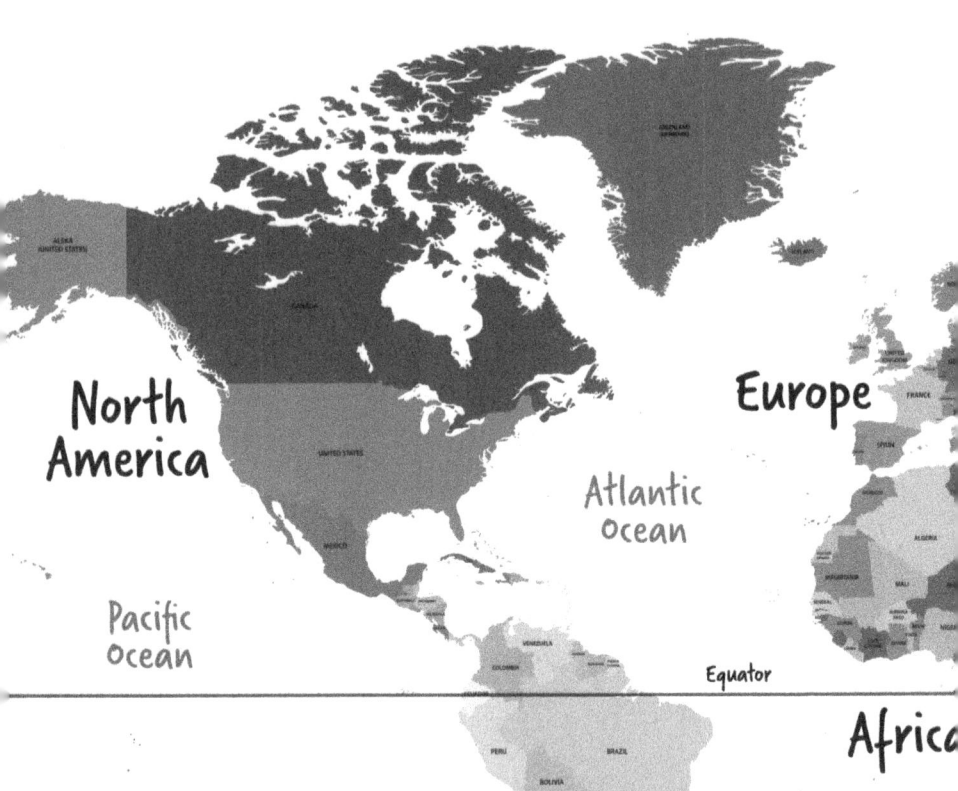

Europe

Atlantic Ocean

Pacific Ocean

Equator

Africa

South America

Southern Ocean

Arctic Ocean

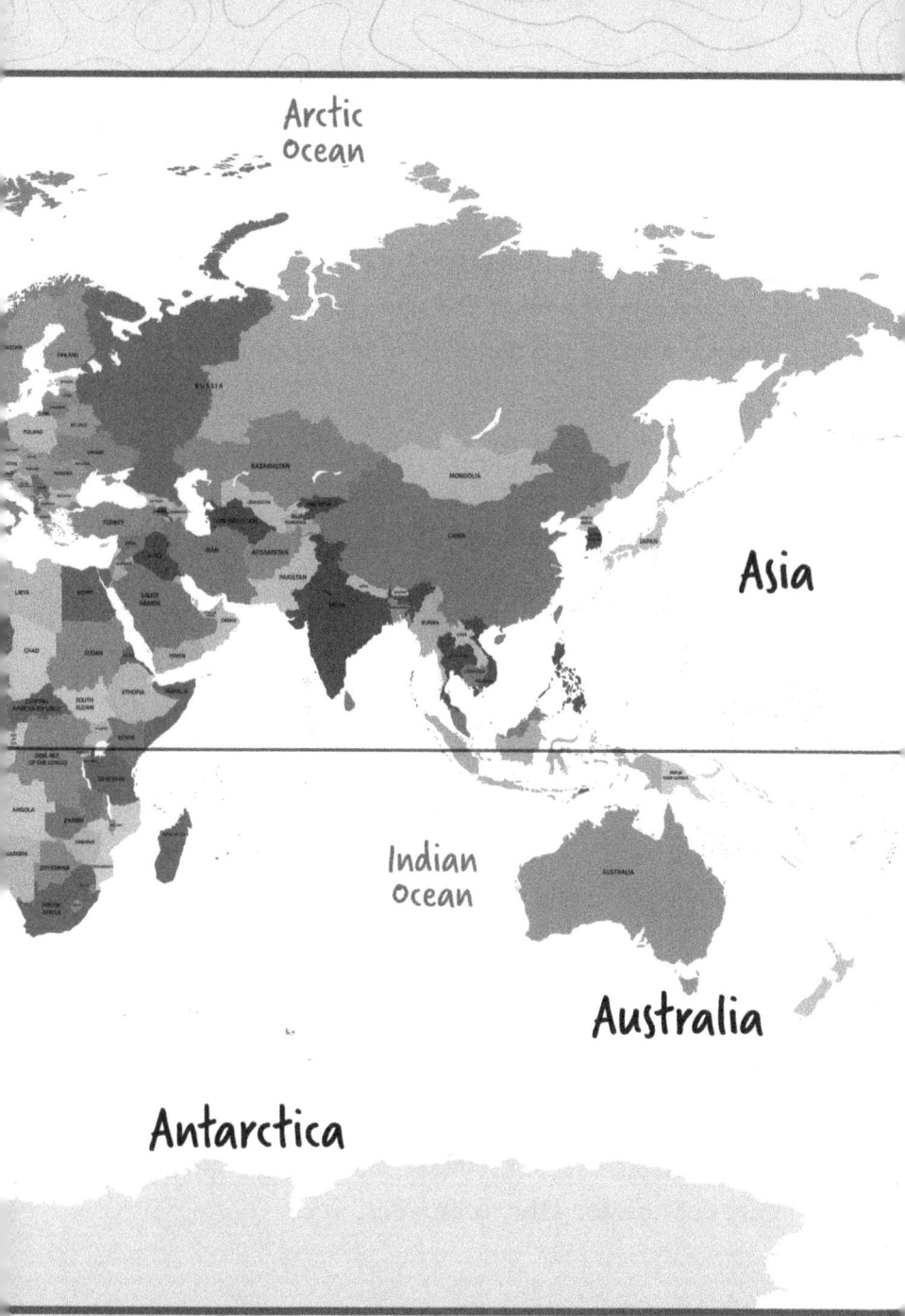

Asia

Indian Ocean

Australia

Antarctica

8. Can you locate the Equator line on the map? It's a special line that divides Earth into the northern and southern hemispheres

9. There are five big oceans on Earth. Can you find any of them on the map? Did you know water covers around 71% of the Earth? That is why we call it the 'blue planet'

Plan your route

Now you know how to navigate like a pro, it's time to plan your first adventure. Use a map book or online map to plan a route for a local adventure. It might be a bike ride to the park, a walk to your friend's house or a walk around your neighbourhood. **No adventure is too small.**

When you have your map, let's use the compass directions we learned. Can you describe the path you'll take using north, south, east and west?

Don't forget to check the scale of the map. Can you figure out how long the route is?

Look for the key on the map. What kind of information does it share? Can you spot any green spaces on the map?

Now, find a perfect spot for a picnic!

Congratulations – you've planned your very first adventure. Now that you know how to use a map, you can explore new horizons, discover hidden wonders and navigate your way to amazing adventures. Get ready to unlock the world's secrets and embark on journeys filled with excitement and discovery!

CHAPTER THREE

BUILD YOUR OWN SHELTER

Are you ready to learn the awesome art of building shelters? Whether you're camping close to home or exploring the wild, having a cosy shelter is like having your very own secret hideout. Let's dive into the world of shelter-building and get you all set for your epic camping adventures!

Do you know why shelters are so important? Well, imagine them as **magical cocoons that keep us safe and cosy**, just like our homes! They protect us from the rain, the wind and the sun. They're our best friends when we're out exploring the world.

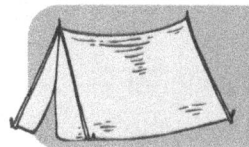

Pitching a tent at the edge of the world

During my travels, I've built all sorts of shelters, each with different challenges and rewards. But by far the most challenging shelter to build was in Antarctica.

Antarctica is a very cold place in the southern hemisphere. Even though it's covered in snow and ice, it's actually a desert! Here's why:

Very little rain: Deserts are places where it hardly ever rains. Well, Antarctica gets very, very little rain – almost as little as a sand desert.

Snow stays: When it snows in Antarctica, it's too cold for the sun to melt it away. It piles up year after year. So even though it has lots of snow and ice, it doesn't make it less of a desert.

Cold and dry: Deserts can be hot, like the Sahara Desert, or cold, like the Arctic tundra. In the case of Antarctica, it's super cold and super dry. That's what makes it a cold desert.

Antarctica is actually the largest desert in the world! The land is covered in ice and snow, and it's very windy there. Sometimes the wind can get so loud that it feels like it's howling all around you. Some people who visit Antarctica choose to wear earplugs when they sleep to help block out the noisy wind and get a good night's rest.

On one snowy day when I was setting up my tent in Antarctica, the wind decided to play a trick on me. As I put the tent pegs into the ground, the wind began to pick up with a loud and wild howling sound. It pushed so hard against my tent that I thought it would fly away!

I was desperately trying to pin my tent down. Just when I thought I had the first peg in place – **whoosh!** – it zoomed up into the air. My tent started wiggling and dancing like it wanted to be a kite!

In an instant, my tent started to lift off the ground. But I wasn't going to let it go on an adventure without me. **I jumped into action fast!** I reached for the flapping tent, grabbed it and wrestled it back down to the ground. It was a big battle, but I won! My tent was safe and sound, back on the ground where it belonged.

I was so worried it might fly away again that I hopped on top of it to hold it down. Thankfully it didn't get blown away.

This adventure taught me something very important – how to be flexible and strong when things don't go as planned and how to **solve a problem under pressure.**

Sometimes, even when we make really good plans, things don't always happen the way we expect. I knew the wind was quite strong but I thought my first peg would hold it down while I tried to secure the rest of the tent! When it didn't, I'm glad I was able to think quickly enough to stop my tent and all my things from flying away.

Building shelters, **just like learning new things in life, is a fun puzzle.** Every time we face a problem, we get better at making our safe and comfy hideouts. And shelters are super important. They keep us warm, safe and cosy, even when we're far away in wild places. And that's why we leap into action if the wind ever threatens to blow them away!

Setting up camp – indoors and outdoors

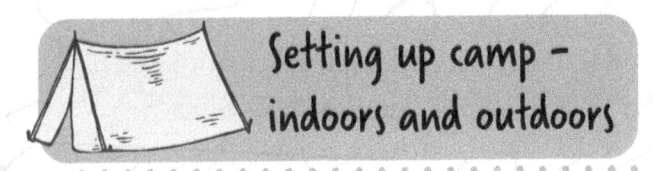

You can start your shelter journey right inside your house! All you need are some blankets and chairs. But don't stop there – you can take your shelter skills outside too. Imagine turning your garden or balcony into a camping wonderland. Just gather lots of blankets, wrap up in layers and bring out sleeping bags or cosy blankets to snuggle in. If you're sleeping outside, a tent is really useful to provide protection from wind and rain.

Build your own den

Now, here is the fun part! Grab some blankets, pillows and chairs and follow the instructions on the next page to create your own secret hideaway.

Step 1: Gather your materials
Ask an adult if it's OK to use items from around your home to build your den. These could be blankets, sheets, pillows and cushions, and don't forget something to secure them like pegs and bungee cords.

Step 2: Choose your location
Find a spot in your home where you want to build your den. It could be in the living room or your bedroom.

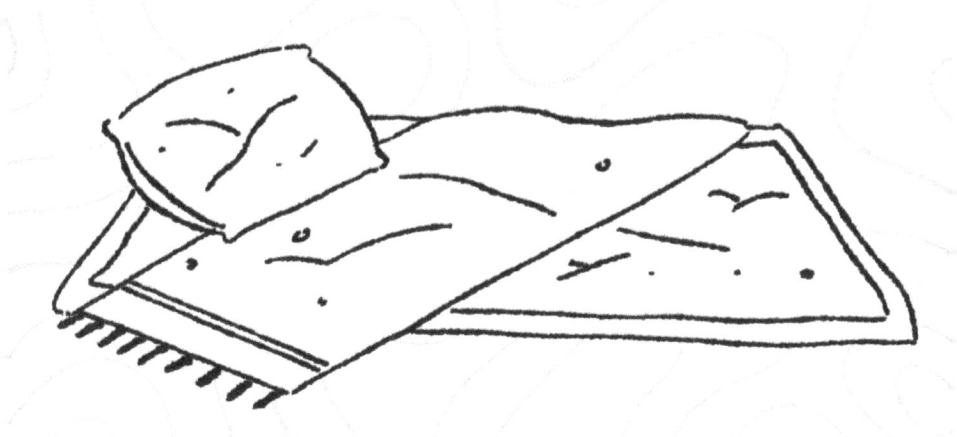

Step 3: Build the base
Start by laying down a few blankets or sheets to create the base of your den. This will be the floor of your cosy space.

Step 4: Create the walls

Drape more blankets or sheets over chairs, tables or other furniture to create the walls of your den. Make sure the walls are sturdy enough to stay in place. You can secure sheets and blankets with clothes pegs to help them stay put.

Step 5: Add comfort

Now it's time to make your den comfy! Place pillows and cushions inside to sit on or lean against, and add your favourite blanket to keep you warm.

Step 6: Personalise your den

Make your den special by adding some of your favourite things. Bring in some stuffed animals, books or even a small torch for reading.

Step 7: Enjoy your den

Once your den is all set up, crawl inside and enjoy your cosy space! You can play games, read stories or just relax. Why not pretend you're camping in the desert or on top of a snowy mountain.

Step 8: Invite friends or family

Don't keep the fun to yourself! Invite your friends, family or even your pets to join you in your awesome den.

Remember, there's no right or wrong way to build your den. Let your creativity run wild and make it a space that feels just right for you. Have a blast building and enjoying your indoor hideaway!

Explorer's top tip

Want to make your den even more special? Grab some colourful fabric or fairy lights to decorate your it. It's like turning your shelter into a magical castle!

Growing your skills

Remember, good adventurers learn from their mistakes. Just like in my Antarctic adventure, where I had to make sure my tent was extra secure the second time around. **It's all about learning and improving.** When you're building a shelter, you've got to think of all the ways it might fall down (or blow away) and make sure you build it strong enough to stay up.

So, brave explorers, now that you've mastered the art of building an indoor den, it's time to take your shelter-building skills to the great outdoors. There's a world of exciting possibilities waiting for you. Whether you're camping in your garden, a campsite or even deep in the woods, knowing how to create a shelter is an essential skill for any young adventurer.

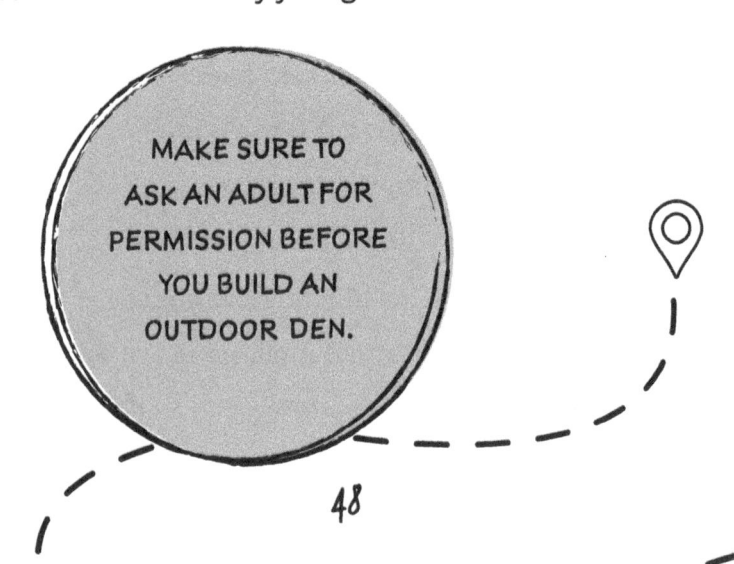

> MAKE SURE TO ASK AN ADULT FOR PERMISSION BEFORE YOU BUILD AN OUTDOOR DEN.

Outdoor shelters

1. **A tent:** Tents are magical fortresses that provide shelter from the elements. Setting up a tent might seem like a puzzle at first, but with practice, you'll become a tent-pitching pro.

2. **Tarp and ropes:** A tarp, short for 'tarpaulin', is like a big, strong blanket made from tough material. You can use ropes to tie tarps together to protect you from rain or provide shade on a sunny day.

3. **Nature:** In the wilderness, you can get creative by using branches to build shelters. Why not try building a shelter by propping up long sticks against each other in a teepee shape.

4. **Sleeping bags and mats:** Don't forget to bring a sleeping bag to snuggle in and a mat to lie on. Keeping warm is key for a good night's sleep.

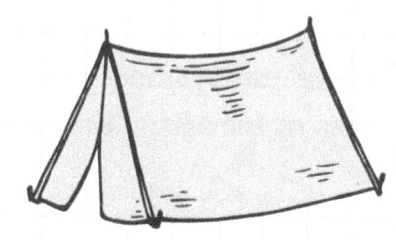

Safety first

Pick a good spot: When you're camping and want to build a shelter, make sure to choose a safe area. Stay away from places like steep cliffs, big lakes or spots where the ground might not be strong.

Weather watch: Keep an eye on the weather. If a big storm is on the way, it's better to wait for another day or find a safe place to stay.

Stay away from fire: Fires are super hot and can be very dangerous. Always remember to stay far away from them. Don't ever touch or get too close to a fire.

Watch for animals: Pay attention to the animals around. Keep your food safe so you don't attract any curious critters to your camp. Animals have a great sense of smell and if they catch a whiff of your snacks, they might come snooping around. Make sure to store your food in secure containers to keep it away from hungry visitors. This way, you can enjoy your camping adventure without any unexpected furry friends joining the party. Keep your treats protected!

Building great memories: As you get better at building shelters, you'll also get more confident in your outdoor adventures. The memories you make while camping, like toasting marshmallows or looking at the stars, will be with you forever. So have fun and stay safe!

Explorer's top tip

Don't build your shelter right next to a source of water like a river. If it's rainy, the river might burst its banks and your shelter might get washed away.

So let your shelter-building adventures take you to new heights. Whether you're constructing a makeshift lean-to in your garden or setting up a tent deep in the wilderness, each shelter you build is a step towards becoming a true outdoor expert.

CHAPTER FOUR
FUELLING UP FOR FUN!

Let's talk about something else that's important — taking care of ourselves while we're out exploring. Master explorers know that you need to have the right fuel to keep your energy up. **Eating a balanced meal of fruits, vegetables, carbohydrates (like pasta), proteins (like meat or tofu) and fats (like cheese) gives us all the energy we need to climb trees, run along sandy beaches and do all the other activities we want to do on our adventures.**

Ready to dive into the world of eating well on your big adventures?

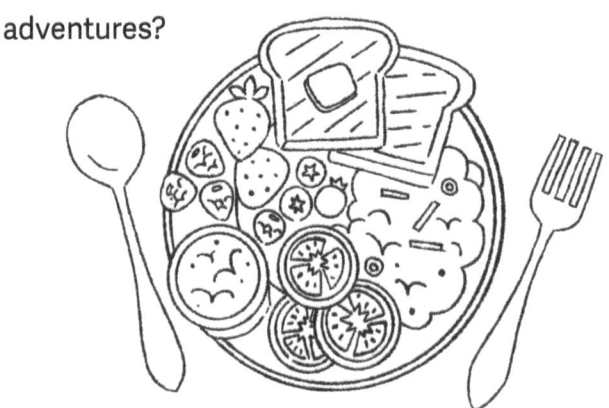

Fuelling the frozen journey

Taking care of ourselves is incredibly important, especially when we embark on exciting adventures. Before I set off for my expedition in Antarctica, I spent a lot of time making sure I had the right foods. I had learned my lesson from my desert marathon and made sure to taste my food well in advance.

I prepared all my food ahead of time, and I even gave it a taste test before my journey. It was essential to include foods that would give me strength and energy. I also packed a good amount of chocolate, because I needed a lot of calories each day while I was out on the icy landscape. **In fact, I ate around 5,000 calories every day.**

In the evenings, I had freeze-dried food – that's food that has been dehydrated so it lasts longer – just like I had during my 156-mile race in the scorching desert. This food starts off like regular food, but it then goes through a dehydrator, which takes all the water out of it, making it lighter and preventing it from going bad. It's much lighter to carry in your backpack and lasts a lot longer than fresh food, so it's perfect for long expeditions.

When it was time to eat, I added some hot water to the freeze-dried food, and like magic, it was ready to eat! My absolute favourite in Antarctica was the pasta bolognese. To cook it, I set up my cooking stuff: a stove, a kettle and some fuel. I used my trusty shovel to cut pieces of snow and melt them back to water in the kettle. After boiling the water, I mixed it with my freeze-dried meal in a pot. In about ten minutes, it was ready to eat. I also treated myself to a yummy hot chocolate every night because it's one of my favourite drinks!

When I was skiing during the day, I didn't have much time to cook. So I packed quick and easy foods in bags. These bags contained chocolate, nuts, raisins and flapjacks. They were different every day to keep things interesting!

I also brought some treats – twenty-five Haribo sweets, to be exact! But I couldn't take too many because I needed to keep my sled from becoming too heavy. During my trip, I savoured those sweets on tough days and even enjoyed a few on Christmas Day!

My adventure in Antarctica lasted seventy days, and I used a lot of energy covering 922 miles. I ate every bit of my food and was running out towards the end.

This meant I had to be careful with my food supply, because I was very hungry!

The food groups

Carbohydrates: Carbohydrates are like power-ups for your body. They give you the energy to keep going. They're found in foods like oats, rice and whole wheat bread. These foods give you long-lasting energy, meaning you can stay active for longer.

Protein: Proteins are like the builders of your body because they help you grow and stay strong, and they keep your body working just right, helping you grow and repair muscles. They're found in foods like beans, nuts and meat. These foods give your muscles the strength they need to swing through the trees and carry your backpack.

Fruits and vegetables: Veggies and fruits are the colourful sidekicks in your food team. They're packed with vitamins and minerals that help you stay healthy and supercharged. Eating these foods gives your body the power to fight off bad germs and help stop you getting sick.

Dairy: Dairy foods help make your bones and teeth strong. They include things like milk, cheese and yogurt. These foods are rich in calcium and help keep your body tough and sturdy.

Fats: Probably your favourite food group, because this includes sweets and chocolate! Fats don't give us a lot of energy, but they taste delicious and help motivate us to keep going. Having cookies, cake or ice cream is a great treat at the end of an adventure. We just can't have too many of them or else we'll feel unwell.

Remember, the key to being a healthy and strong explorer is to **eat a little bit from each of these food groups**. Your body needs a mixture of all these different foods to stay in tip-top shape and ready for any adventure that comes your way.

A good explorer's breakfast

Just like how an explorer plans their route, you can plan your meals for when you're on your adventure. Imagine mapping out your breakfast, lunch and dinner. What are you going to have? Consider whether you want to cook every meal or have some ready to go like I did in Antarctica.

Mealtimes are also a good time to check in with yourself. **How do you feel today? Are you full of energy?** If not, it might be time to fuel up with some delicious and nutritious food.

So let's map out an adventure breakfast plate! See if you can get all the food groups in there.

To give you some ideas, I've written what I would have on my plate.

Think of your breakfast plate as your explorer's fuel, giving you the energy and nutrients you need for your adventures. What are you going to put on your plate?

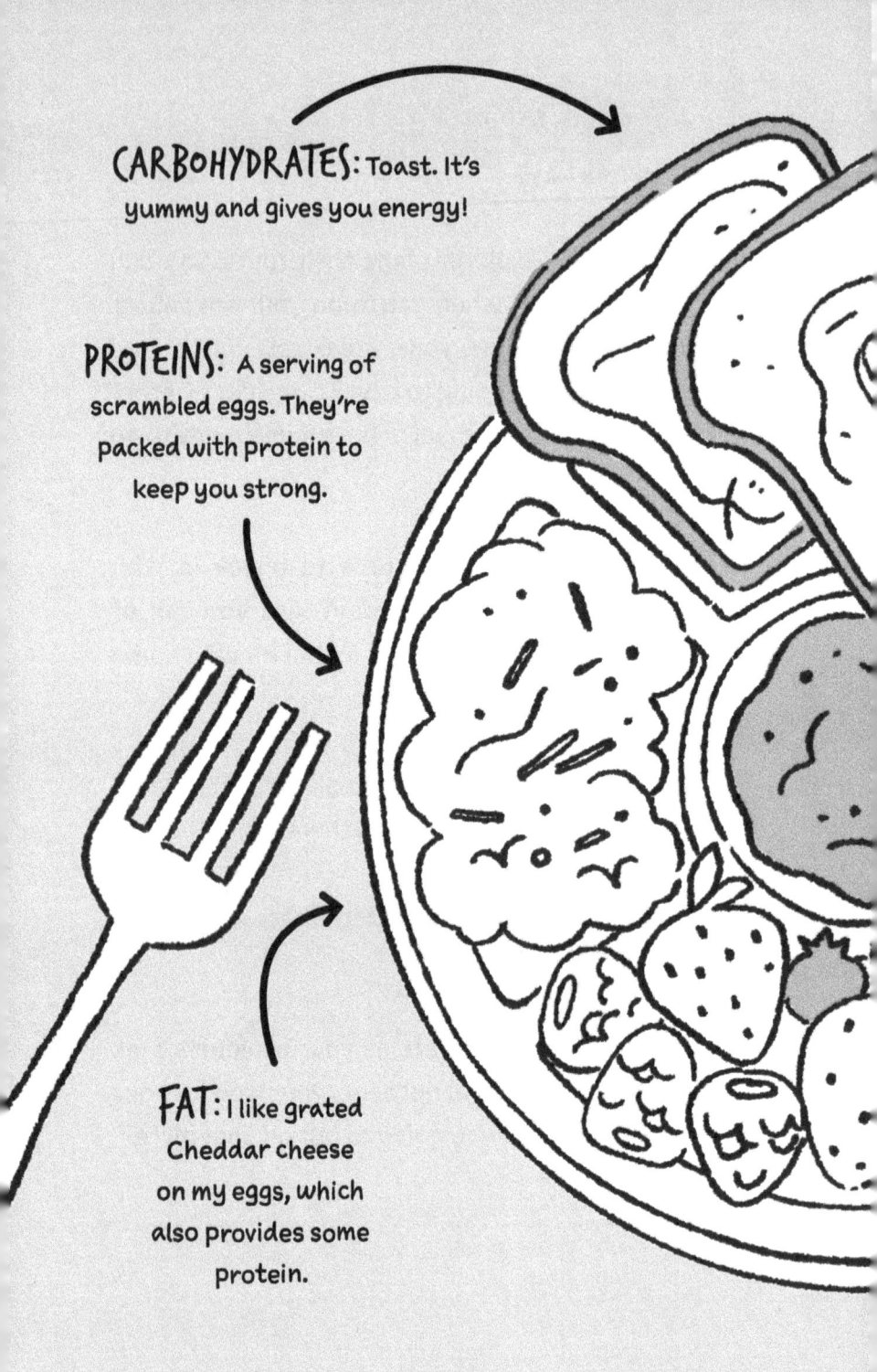

CARBOHYDRATES: Toast. It's yummy and gives you energy!

PROTEINS: A serving of scrambled eggs. They're packed with protein to keep you strong.

FAT: I like grated Cheddar cheese on my eggs, which also provides some protein.

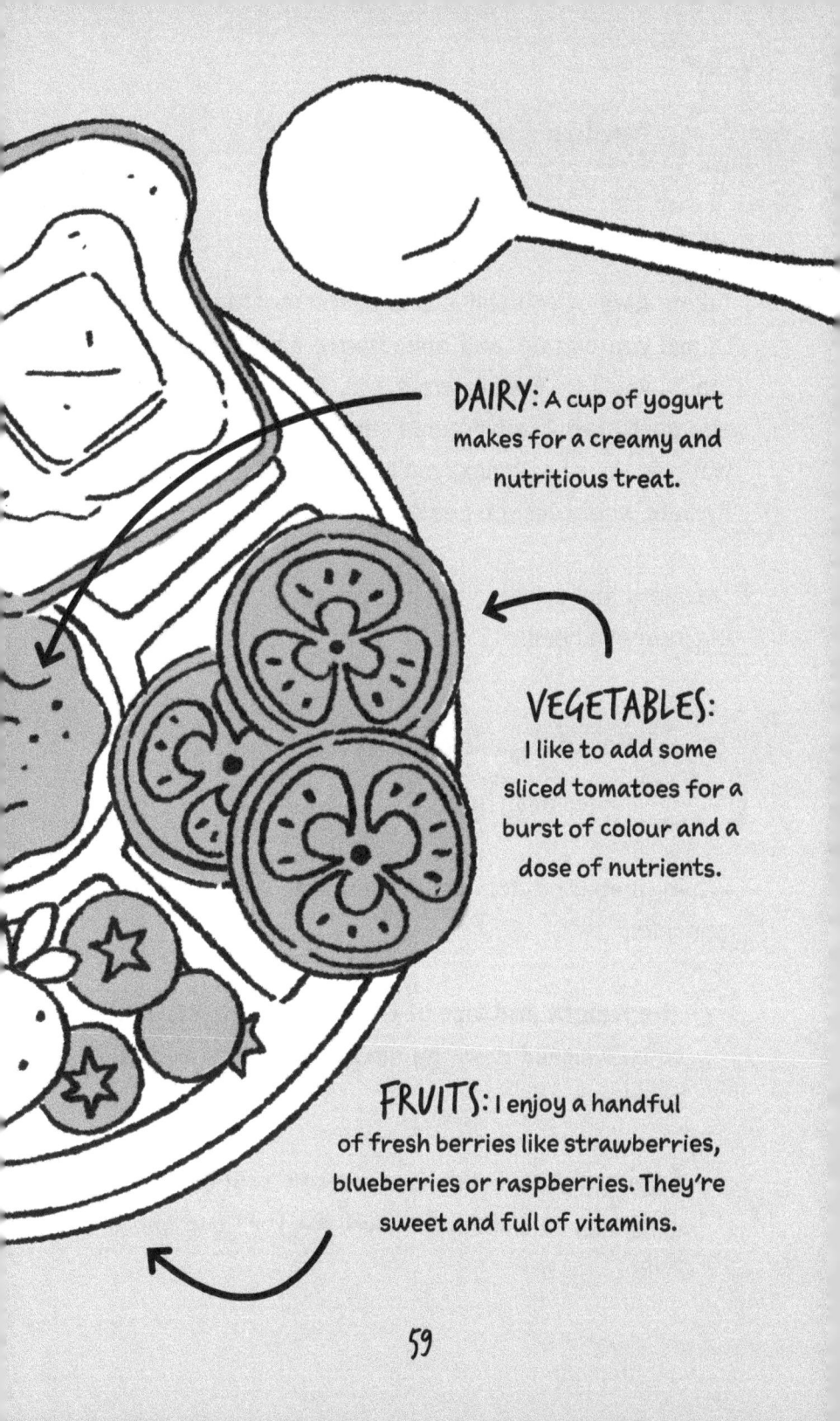

DAIRY: A cup of yogurt makes for a creamy and nutritious treat.

VEGETABLES: I like to add some sliced tomatoes for a burst of colour and a dose of nutrients.

FRUITS: I enjoy a handful of fresh berries like strawberries, blueberries or raspberries. They're sweet and full of vitamins.

Embrace the adventure of eating well

Taking care of yourself is one of the most important things you can do, and once you're eating the right foods, you'll be feeling great too. You'll have lots of energy for your adventures, and with snacks and water in your backpack, you'll be able to fuel up and hydrate whenever you need.

Now let's fuel up, have fun and get ready for the next big journey ahead!

How to pack food for an expedition

When preparing for any adventure, you need to consider:

The weight and size of the food: You don't want to be weighed down by heavy food like a bag of potatoes.

Expiry dates: Fresh food doesn't stay good for very long, so make sure it will last for your whole trip.

Whether you need to assemble the food: You don't want to have to spend a lot of time and energy preparing food when you're on the go, so bring foods that are already prepared, like a sandwich.

What your favourite foods are: Pack foods that you know you'll enjoy eating.

How much you need to drink: It's important to stay hydrated on adventures. Always pack a bottle of water and avoid sugary drinks, as they can dehydrate you.

Explorer's top tip

Want to know something cool? Our bodies are over 50% water, but we still get thirsty. We need water to stay healthy and strong. So make sure you're sipping water throughout the day to keep yourself hydrated.

Listen to your body

Your body knows just what you need, so make sure you listen to it. Tummy rumbling? You're hungry. Dry mouth? You're thirsty. Feeling dizzy? Time for a sit down in the shade. Don't wait until you're feeling tired or hungry to refuel – **let your body guide you.**

Get foody

My favourite part of any exploration is trying new foods and sharing meals with my fellow explorers. Food tells us lots about different cultures and the particular resources of different countries. Next time you're on an adventure with a friend, why not make your favourite snack for them and have them make you their favourite in return. Do you think you'll both make the same thing?

GRAB A PIECE OF PAPER AND DRAW YOUR FAVOURITE SNACK.

Make or buy: Did you make this snack yourself or is it something you bought? Share the cooking adventure or the joy of discovering it in a store with a friend.

Ingredients: What makes your snack so delicious? It's the ingredients! What is your snack made from? Is there something bitter in it like lemon? Or sweet like my favourite treat – Haribos!

Food groups: Explore the different food groups your snack belongs to. Is it a mix of several groups, or does it fit into one particular category?

Now you know all about the food groups, have planned your healthy breakfast and know how to pack your snacks! Remember, taking care of your body with good food and staying hydrated is all part of what makes a great adventurer. Just like your gear and maps, your meals are an essential part of your toolkit for exploring the world. **So pack healthy foods, listen to your body and have fun!**

CHAPTER FIVE

GET OUTDOORS!

Now that you're prepared for your adventure, are you ready to step into the amazing world of nature? Exploring the outdoors is like opening a treasure chest filled with wonders waiting to be discovered. You never know what animals you might see along the way, what trees you might climb and what insects might flit across your path. That's half the excitement! But remember, **a good explorer shows respect for new lands and creatures.** We share this planet with lots of beautiful plants and animals, and so we must take care of it and leave no trace we were here.

Why nature deserves our respect

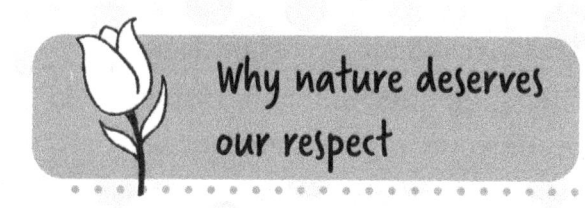

I once went on an extraordinary journey to a land where animals freely roam and breathtaking landscapes unfold endlessly: Kenya. A beautiful country nestled in the captivating continent of Africa.

As I set foot on the African soil, I couldn't contain my excitement. It was my first time visiting this incredible place, and little did I know I was about to witness the most extraordinary sight of all – **animals in their natural habitats.**

Imagine this: vast, open plains where the golden savannah met the endless sky. The sun beamed down warmly, casting a golden hue on the landscape. And there, in the distance, a gentle giant appeared – an elephant, majestic and free. It was a sight to behold, unlike anything I'd ever seen before.

But the elephants were only the beginning. As I journeyed deeper into the heart of Kenya, I crossed paths with towering giraffes, their graceful necks reaching high into the trees nibbling on leaves, and racing zebras roaming freely.

It was in Kenya that **I learned an important lesson – the significance of gentleness and respect**. Just like meeting someone new, interacting with these incredible creatures required a soft approach. Observing them from a distance, understanding their behaviours and appreciating their unbridled freedom became my focus.

Growing up in the UK, I was used to seeing these animals in zoos, not in the wild. And as important as it is that these animals are protected in conservations and zoos, there's nothing like seeing them in their natural habitat.

Exploring new environments

Nature is a magical playground with lots of different places to explore. There are tall mountains, lush forests, sandy deserts and sparkling oceans. Each place has its own rules, like how to navigate a mountain trail or how to enjoy the waves at the beach. When you're in a new environment, take a moment to observe how others act. Are they avoiding walking on the grass and sticking to the paths? Are they making sure not to pick the flowers? Some places, like national parks and protected areas, have rules for how you act in them. They usually have signs, but if not, these basic rules should help you.

- **Stick to the paths:** Whenever you're out exploring, try to stay on the paths or trails that are already there. This helps protect the homes of plants and animals.

- **Leave nature as you found it:** Nature is a bit like a museum and we don't take things from museums, right? So remember, don't pick flowers, rocks or leaves, even if they're pretty. Leave everything just the way you found it.

Safety first: Wear a helmet while biking, wear a life jacket on a boat and apply sunscreen to protect your skin from the sun's rays. Safety gear is important for a reason – it keeps you safe.

Respect others: There might be other people enjoying the space, so make sure to give them plenty of room to wander and don't be too noisy. Everyone is allowed to explore nature.

Nature bathing

No, it's not having a bath outdoors! Nature bathing is all about enjoying being outside. Why not have a go?

Find a cosy spot outdoors and sit comfortably. Close your eyes and listen.

Can you hear the birds singing, the wind whispering or the leaves rustling? Nature has its own magical music and you're a part of it too.

Can you smell the freshly cut grass or something tasty cooking on a campfire nearby?

📍 What can you feel under your fingertips? Stones, sand, dirt?

📍 What can you taste? Have you just had a delicious snack?

📍 And lastly, open your eyes. What can you see around you? Is it sunny or cloudy?

📍 Well done. You've had your first nature bath. What did you think?

Nature bathing is a great way to connect with the Earth and take in all the brilliant things happening around you. **Exploring isn't just about moving – it's about using all your senses to connect with the world.** I love doing this when I'm outside, closing my eyes and experiencing things in a different way.

Explorer's top tip

Want to be a nature hero? Bring a bin bag with you next time you go for a walk. With the help of a grown-up, pick up any rubbish you find along your walk. At the end, put it all in a bin. This small action will make a huge difference, as animals can hurt themselves on our rubbish and it can ruin their habitats.

Adapting and growing

As an adventurer, you must learn adapt to new places. Here's how you can adapt to some of the different places you might go exploring.

Camping in the woods: Imagine you're going on a camping trip to a dense forest. It's a new place with unfamiliar sounds and creatures. Adapting means setting up a cosy campsite, learning about the animals and adjusting to the night-time forest noises.

Beach adventure: If you're going to the beach, adapting involves getting used to the sand, waves and seagulls. Paddle in the salty ocean water, build sandcastles and learn about the tides. Sometimes, you may need to change your plans if the weather becomes windy or rainy.

Mountain hike: Going on a mountain hike means adapting to heights and cooler temperatures. You'll need to plan your breaks and dress warmly. Adapting also includes being aware of wildlife like squirrels and birds in the mountains.

Garden camp-out: Even camping in your own garden can be an adventure. Adapting might mean getting used to sleeping in a tent and identifying the sounds of the night creatures like crickets and owls.

Adapting to new places can be exciting and fun. Once you're used to different environments, you'll feel prepared for anything.

The magic of nature

What's the best part about exploring new places? You never know what you'll find! Nature is full of surprises, from chirping birds to hidden flowers. So why not document all the brilliant animals and beautiful plants you come across?

Bring a notebook with you on your next adventure and draw all the insects, animals, plants and people you see. This could be anything! How about the tallest tree you've seen? Or the tiniest insect? Or a leaf with lots of lines on it...

If you enjoyed that, then why not try some of the other activities I like to do when I'm out exploring?

📍 **Nature art:** Nature can be your canvas. Use rocks, leaves or sticks to create beautiful art in the great outdoors. Become a nature artist and your artwork will make others smile.

📍 **Nature's lullaby:** When you're camping under the starry sky, listen to the sounds of nature as it lulls you to sleep. Crickets, frogs and gentle winds are nature's own bedtime story.

📍 **The tiniest explorers:** If you have younger siblings or friends, be a guide to the tiny explorers. Teach them about nature's wonders, help them discover insects and show them how to be respectful explorers too.

📍 **Nature journal:** Start a nature journal where you can record your outdoor adventures and write down your thoughts and observations. Your journal will become a treasure trove of memories.

📍 **Create a mini nature library:** Collect books about nature and create a mini outdoor library in your garden or on your balcony. You can read about the creatures and plants you encounter and learn even more.

And most importantly...

Share your nature adventures: Just like you share your toys with friends, share your nature discoveries with others. Tell them about the cool animals you saw or the fascinating plants you found. Be a nature storyteller.

And remember, you can learn about nature at home too. Why not ask a grown-up to help you find the animals you've discovered on the internet or in a book? There's so much to learn about these creatures and their habitats.

Get outdoors

So, my curious adventurers, are you ready to get outdoors? You've learned the rules and discovered nature bathing and loads of other activities you can do once you're out and about. You don't even need to remember them all – just bring this book with you!

Remember to respect the Earth, animals and plants you meet on your travels. Leave no trace that you've been there – this means picking up all your rubbish.

CHAPTER SIX
SUPER SURVIVAL SKILLS

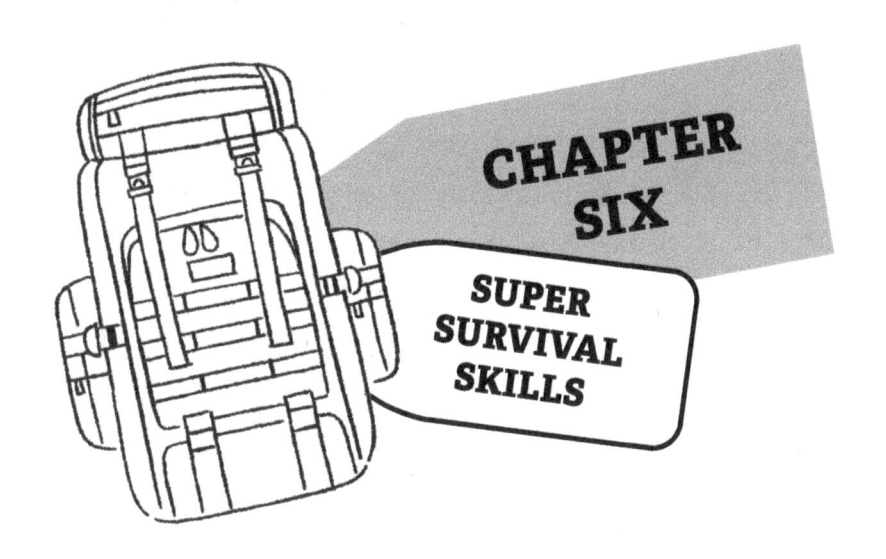

Ready to learn some incredible survival skills? Being an adventurer means being prepared for anything. So when things don't go to plan you need to know how to avoid danger and get help. So let's dive into the world of staying safe, making plans and embracing challenges. Get ready to become your very own hero.

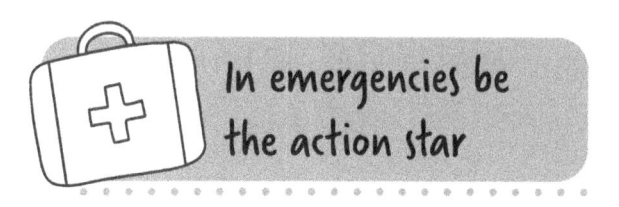

In emergencies be the action star

In Greenland, I once had an incredible adventure with my Norwegian guide, Are. Firstly, I want to explain that Greenland isn't all green! It's actually quite the opposite. You see, Greenland is a massive icy island. So when you think of Greenland, picture huge icebergs, snow-capped mountains and vast icy plains. It's a land of incredible frozen beauty and epic adventures, but you need a warm coat and your explorer's spirit to explore its icy wonders.

This trip was a big one for me, lasting twenty-seven days. Our adventure started with a rocky boat ride. We went past some of these amazing icebergs, but I was feeling a little seasick. Don't worry – I felt much better once we got on land.

At first, we had to hike for a couple of days while carrying our gear before we reached the icy and snowy areas. This part of our journey was challenging because it rained continuously for days. And to make things even more difficult, we had to navigate around lots of crevasses. Crevasses are huge cracks in the icy ground, and they can be quite scary to cross. My heart skipped a beat a few times as we made our way over them.

After successfully crossing the crevasse fields, we found ourselves on snowy ground. But just when we thought things were getting easier, a powerful storm hit us. We knew the storm was coming, but it arrived a bit earlier than expected. To protect ourselves, we had to build big snow walls around our tent. But by the time we got the tent set up, we were pretty wet, and my gear was damp. I even had trouble unzipping my **jacket because it had frozen shut!** Are helped me with that. Inside the tent, we made a plan and called our safety team using satellite phones. After spending a few days in the storm, we decided to finish our trip early. Having a plan and taking action is important in these situations. We put up the tent quickly and made that call to our safety team as soon as we were warm and safe inside. It was quite a scary adventure!

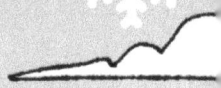

Asking for help

Let's discuss an important survival skill – knowing when to ask for help. It's not just OK to ask for help; it's crucial in certain situations. Imagine needing to start a fire to stay warm or finding shelter to protect yourself from the elements – these are essential expedition skills. But you know what's equally important? **Recognising when you need help and asking for it.** It's OK to tell your adventurer friends that you could use a hand. In all my adventures, I make sure I have a way to contact people in case I ever need assistance, and that's a smart and responsible thing to do. So always remember, knowing when to ask for help is a crucial skill that all good explorers need.

Adventure puzzles

Want to test your explorer senses? Ask a grown-up to hide something small in your home. Now it's time to put your detective skills to the test. While searching, pay close attention to everything around you. What do you see? What looks different from usual? How does the environment change as you get closer to the hidden object? Being an explorer means being super aware of your surroundings.

After you find the hidden item, tell the grown-up what you observed during your hunt. This way, you'll learn to be even more alert when exploring – a key survival skill for any young adventurer!

Explorer's top tip

If you ever fall into in cold water, float like a starfish on your back. When we're very cold, our bodies go into shock and we find it hard to swim. If you float on your back, you can breathe deeply and let your body calm down until you're able to get out of the water. Just like a starfish riding the waves, you've got this!

Staying safe and avoiding trouble

Adventure is awesome, but **safety comes first**. There are things we need to avoid in order to stay out of trouble. For example, we should never go near wild animals. They might feel threatened by us being so close to them and charge at us. Their instinct is to attack because they're just as scared as we are and when we're scared, we don't think properly. Learning to make safe choices is a powerful tool in your adventure toolkit.

Top tips for avoiding trouble

The buddy system: This is something I learned in the Army. You partner up with one person, your buddy, and you're both responsible for each other's safety. You have to stick together as a team. It's a way to make sure that no one is alone during tasks and it keeps us all safe. You should always tell an adult where you're going as well.

Step light, keep quiet: This was another thing I learned when I was out on exercise with the Army. I did not want to be loud and draw attention to myself. When you're out in the wild and you're worried that there's a dangerous animal near you, walk softly (step light) to avoid disturbing animals and try to be silent (keep quiet) until you're a safe distance away. Always remember, how you behave around animals depends on the type of animal and where you are. Sometimes, making noise or using special sounds can let animals know you're around, so you don't surprise them. Ask an adult about the rules for the area you're in, pay attention to what's happening around you and use your good judgement based on the kind of animals and the place you're exploring.

Know your 3 Ws: Always let someone know WHO you're going with, WHAT you're doing and WHERE you're going, so they can find you in case you get lost.

Follow the rules, use your tools: Just like in school, follow safety rules, and remember to use the tools you have (like a compass or torch) when needed.

When in doubt, shout it out: If you ever feel lost or scared, don't hesitate to shout for help or make a loud noise to attract attention.

📍 **Keep a plan, no matter the land:** Always have a plan for your adventure, whether it's in the mountains, the forest or even your own garden.

📍 **Stay low, go slow:** If you ever find yourself in a situation where there is fire, remember to stay close to the ground (low) and move carefully (slow) to stay safe.

📍 **Dress right, stay tight:** Dress appropriately for the weather (dress right) and keep your group together (stay tight) to prevent accidents and stay warm.

📍 **Stay smart, keep your distance:** When you encounter animals in the wild, stay smart by observing them from a safe distance. Remember, animals are just like us, and they prefer their space too. It's important to respect their homes and let them be.

📍 **Weather watch:** Keep an eye on the sky and listen to the wind. Nature sends us clues about what's coming. If it looks stormy, find shelter.

📍 **Stay hydrated:** Your body needs water, so keep sipping, especially when it's hot outside.

First aid

Knowing some basic first aid skills will help you go from novice explorer to master adventurer. Learning how to treat cuts, scrapes and rashes can come in handy when you're out in the wild. You can patch up your fellow explorers and save the day!

Before you try and do any of these things, make sure to first tell an adult so they can help you.

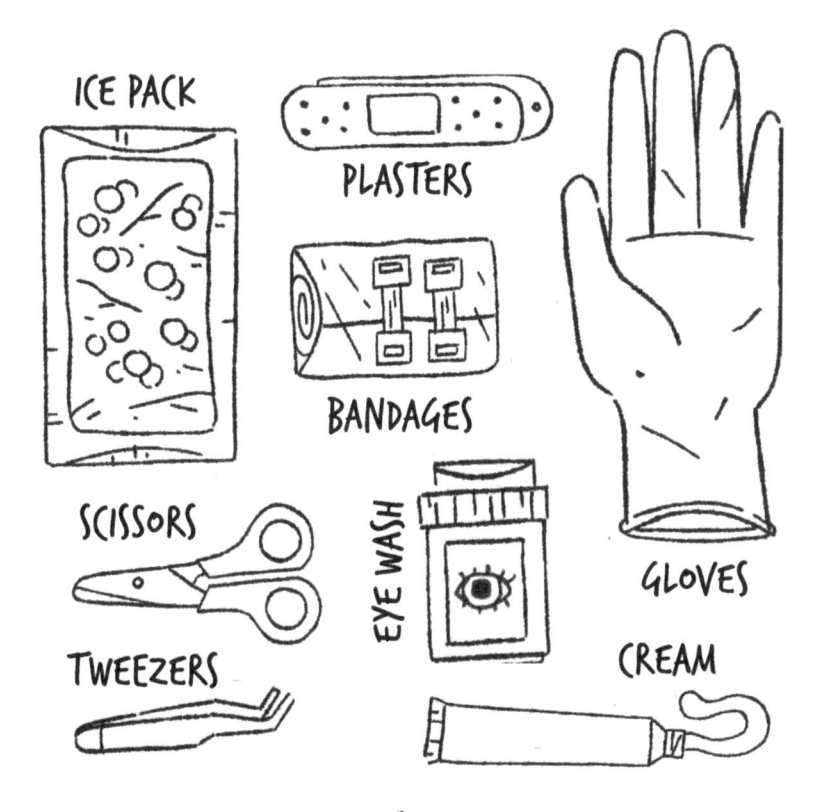

ICE PACK

PLASTERS

BANDAGES

SCISSORS

EYE WASH

GLOVES

TWEEZERS

CREAM

📍 **Cuts and scrapes:** If you get a cut or scrape, wash it gently with clean water. You can use a bandage or a clean cloth to cover it. If it's a big cut and keeps bleeding, ask an adult for help.

📍 **Bee stings or insect bites:** If a bee stings you or you get an insect bite, ask an adult to remove the stinger or help you clean the bite. Putting an ice pack on it can help with the pain and swelling.

📍 **Bruises:** If you get a bruise from a bump or fall, put an ice pack or a clean cloth with cold water on it. It might make the bruise feel better.

📍 **Sprains or twists:** If you twist your ankle or hurt a joint, rest the area and put an ice pack on it. You can ask an adult for help if it hurts a lot.

📍 **Burns:** If you touch something hot and get a burn, run it under cold water for a few minutes. An adult can decide if you need more help.

📍 **Nosebleeds:** If your nose starts bleeding, pinch your nostrils together and lean forward, not backward. It helps stop the bleeding faster.

Allergies: If you know you're allergic to something, like nuts or certain foods, be careful not to eat them. Always tell an adult if you eat something you're allergic to. They can help you get the right medicine.

Remember, if you're not sure what to do when you're hurt or not feeling well, find an adult you trust, like your parents, a teacher or a caregiver. They can help you and make sure you get the right care.

Embrace challenges

Just like in an action movie, your life is full of exciting twists and turns. If you face a tough challenge, take it one step at a time. Break it into smaller pieces, like I did in Greenland. **Breathe, stay calm and remind yourself you're OK.** And you know what? You're amazing, and you can handle anything. This will help you catch your breath and think clearly about what to do next.

What would you do in each of these scenarios?

Scenario 1: You're lost in the woods, and it's getting dark. What should you do?
A) Call for help and use your torch to attract attention
B) Keep walking in the dark to find your way out

Scenario 2: You come across a snake while hiking. What's the best action to take?
A) Stay still and slowly back away from the snake
B) Try to pick up the snake to get a closer look

Scenario 3: Your path is cut off by a river. You don't know how deep it is or how strong the current is. What do you do?
A) Risk it and try to swim into the river
B) Keep walking and find a safe way to cross

Scenario 4: You're camping, and you see dark clouds and hear thunder. What's the safest thing to do?
A) Stay in your tent to keep dry
B) Find shelter in a building or a car to avoid lightning

Scenario 5: You find some colourful berries in the wild. How should you react?
A) Eat them right away. They look tasty!
B) Avoid eating them because they might be poisonous

Scenario 6: You're hiking in the mountains, and you suddenly realise you don't know which trail to take. What's the best thing to do?
A) Stop, retrace your steps and try to find any trail markers or signs
B) Keep walking and hope you find the right path

Scenario 7: You're at the beach and you notice the water is pulling you out to sea. What should you do?
A) Try to swim against the current to get back to shore
B) Float on your back and wave for help

Scenario 8: You're outside in chilly weather and you start feeling very cold. What should you do to stay warm?
A) Remove your warm clothing layers
B) Put on extra clothing, like a jacket or hat

Find the answers on page 186.

When to call emergency services

If you ever come across something really, really bad and you need immediate help, **call 999**. You'll be able to speak to someone who can help you and this will save the day when someone is hurt or something dangerous is happening. You should call 999 if someone is badly hurt, there's a big fire or you see something very, very wrong. But remember, **only use 999 when it's a real emergency** because the people on the other end of the line are there to help when things are extremely serious – scraping your knee doesn't count. Try and tell an adult before you call 999, as they can call for you, but if there isn't an adult around it's better to call them than try and fix the situation by yourself.

999 is an important number to know, but only use it when you really need it.

CHAPTER SEVEN

EMBRACE MISTAKES

You're bound to make lots of mistakes when you first start exploring. Even the bravest explorers, like me, have had moments when things didn't go as planned. We forget to peg our tents down properly, pack disgusting food or forget some of our kit. It happens to everyone. But there's **a lot we can learn from our mistakes**. Let's unlock the secret power of failure, learn how to bounce back and turn every adventure into a treasure trove of wisdom.

Why failing is totally normal

The first time I went to Antarctica, my trip went to plan. I completed 700 miles to the South Pole in forty days. The second time, my aim was to cross the whole of Antarctica. It was a huge goal and unfortunately I did not complete it. **I ended up over 100 miles away from where I wanted to be. I was so disappointed.**

During my second trip, I spent seventy days on the expedition, pulling my heavy sled filled with gear and equipment. That sled weighed a whopping 120 kg, and dragging it through the snowy wilderness was really, really hard. The weather was often rough, especially at the start of my journey. I faced strong winds that could go up to nearly 60 mph!

I had a lot of distance to cover (over 1,000 miles) and only seventy days to complete it. This meant I needed to cover a certain distance each day. But I wasn't travelling as far as I had hoped to each day, and I quickly fell behind schedule. The snowy terrain was full of these funny-shaped ridges and my sled had a habit of tipping over. It was quite a task to get it back in the right position! I realised eventually that I wouldn't be able to catch up and reach my end point. I was devastated. I'd had this big goal in mind, and **now it seemed impossible to achieve.**

But then something changed. I remembered why I had come to Antarctica in the first place. It wasn't just about that final destination. My main goal was to push my own limits and inspire others to do the same. And you know what? I had definitely pushed my own boundaries! **So I learned that it's OK to fail sometimes.** Failure taught me a lot about myself. It showed me that I could keep going, even when things were incredibly tough. I discovered my own strength and resilience and that was so freeing.

Even if I had known I was going to fail, I would still have gone on this expedition because it taught me so much about my own resilience. When I finally finished, it took me a while to fully come to terms with not completing the journey. I'd also injured my leg so I had to spend time healing and letting my body recover from the gruelling expedition. Patience was key, and I had to be kind to myself.

Bouncing back and finding your way

When things get tough, **remember why you started your adventure.** Dig deep and find your courage, and remind yourself that you're here because you're brave, curious and ready to explore. So how can you bounce back from challenges? Well, here are a few practical things you can do:

Ask for help: It's perfectly fine to reach out to grown-ups or friends when you need help.

Remind yourself of your strengths: You have amazing qualities and talents. Take a moment to think about what you're good at and what makes you unique. This can boost your confidence and help you overcome obstacles.

Take one step at a time: Big challenges can seem overwhelming. But, like climbing a mountain, you don't have to reach the summit in one giant leap. Break your challenge into smaller, manageable steps. With each step, you'll get closer to your goal.

Never give up on yourself: No matter how tough it may seem, the most important thing is to never give up on yourself even if that means giving up on your goal. Every adventure has its ups and downs and sometimes you have to accept that what you set out to do isn't going to happen. This isn't a failure but a clever choice to accept that your adventure can't be achieved on that day and to try again on another.

Lessons learned

The next time you make a mistake, why not try this challenge to help you come to terms with it.

Write down the mistake you made in a notebook or on a piece of paper. Maybe you were unkind to a friend or didn't plan your route properly and got lost on an adventure.

What happened?

How did it make you feel?

Sometimes, when I make a mistake, I feel a bit embarrassed and even think that I'm the only one who's ever felt that way.

What can you learn from this mistake? Did it teach you an important lesson?

Making mistakes is something we all do and it's perfectly OK. Everyone makes mistakes from time to time.

What would you do differently next time?

When I make a mistake, I try to be better prepared for next time but I also cut myself some slack and remind myself that mistakes are a natural part of life. It's essential to forgive ourselves and keep moving forward. That way, our brains can focus on finding solutions instead of dwelling on the errors. Making mistakes can actually help us become even better adventurers!

How do you feel now? Was writing about your mistake helpful? Do you feel better about it?

Making mistakes is a great opportunity for us to learn something new. Now your brain will think about the solutions to the problem rather than feeling bad about it.

Explorer's top tip

Someone once gave me a great piece of advice – treat yourself like you would treat your best friend. So I was kinder to myself and I forgave myself!

You're not the only one who makes mistakes

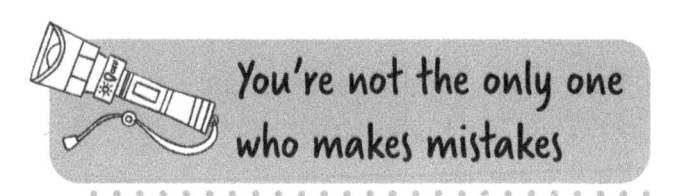

We all do, and some people's mistakes have led to amazing achievements. Did you know...

◉ The Wright brothers, who invented the aeroplane, had to try a lot of different things before they finally made the first successful flight. They made mistakes in how they designed the wings, how they controlled the plane and even in the engine. It took them a while to figure out the right combination of things that would make a plane fly the way they wanted. So they learned from each mistake and kept trying until they got it right!

◉ The Deinonychus dinosaur was discovered in Wyoming, USA by complete accident. A palaeontologist found the fossilised bones while looking for another dinosaur.

◉ Astronomers Arno Penzias and Robert Wilson accidentally discovered the Big Bang when listening to a strange noise coming through their antenna from space. This buzzing was the leftover radiation from the Big Bang.

📍 The Viking Explorer Naddodd only discovered Iceland because his ship was blown off course on his journey from Norway to the Faroe Islands.

Guess what? **Failing can lead to some of the coolest discoveries. Failure sometimes shows us a new path.** I didn't reach my goal in Antarctica, but I learned so much along the way. Every step teaches you something new.

> Embrace your mistakes

Every explorer faces challenges. **Failure is a test to see how strong and creative you are.** It just shows that you're trying something new. I've failed at lots of things too, but I'm so glad I tried them. They made me stronger and smarter.

Move on

It is important to forgive yourself when you make a mistake. What matters is how you learn from them and move on. **Focus on the positive aspects of your experience**, such as what you learned or how you grew as a person.

Here are a few of the things I find helpful after I have made a mistake:

- **Talk to your friends, your parents or a teacher.** They'll help you find the funny side.

- **Don't give up.** If you keep trying, you will eventually learn from your mistakes and achieve your goals.

- **Celebrate your successes.** When you do learn from your mistakes and achieve your goals, be sure to celebrate your success. This will help you stay motivated and keep moving forward.

CHAPTER EIGHT

THE BEST ADVENTURES ARE WITH FRIENDS!

Hey there, adventure buddies! Did you know that the coolest adventures are even more amazing when you do them with friends? Yep, it's true! Let's dive into the world of group adventures, where teamwork makes everything more fun, exciting and memorable. Get ready to learn why friends are the best companions on any journey.

Why adventures are always better together

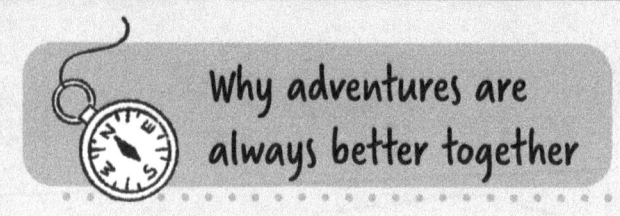

I once did a challenge where I did step-ups for 24 hours to support the hard-working medical staff in the NHS. This was during the COVID pandemic when all medical professionals were going above and beyond, so I wanted to show them my appreciation. And the best part about this challenge was that I wasn't alone. My friends from all around the world joined in virtually. **We were a global adventure team!**

I did the challenge in my garden with just one step. It might not seem like much, but it's a stepping stone to an amazing journey. With snacks by my side and the support of my adventure buddies, I started at 12 p.m. I wasn't in a hurry – I took it slow, one step at a time.

As I stepped up and down that single step, something magical happened. I started receiving videos from friends everywhere, doing their own step-ups. It was like a virtual adventure parade, with each person bringing their own energy and excitement. **Together, we were unstoppable!**

My adventure team were a diverse bunch. We had people of all ages, from six-month-old babies (held by their parents, of course) to adults like me doing step-ups in their gardens or homes. One friend went all out, wearing different animal costumes as she tackled her stairs at home. Many of my friends created signs to encourage me and keep my motivation high.

Then came the midnight hours, the time when the world is quiet and the stars are your companions. Between 2 a.m. and 4 a.m., things got tough, but I didn't give up. With each step, **I reminded myself that challenges are like puzzles – you solve them one piece at a time.**

When the clock struck 12 p.m. the next day, I was finished! My legs were aching a lot and I was very tired, but too excited to go to sleep straight away. And the best part? Together, we raised a lot of money for charity. It was a **monumental achievement**, showcasing the power of teamwork and the support of amazing friends. The virtual adventure turned into a celebration, and I couldn't have done it without my fantastic adventure team!

The aches in my legs lasted for about a week but I didn't care. I had finished my step-ups and raised a lot of money for charity, so it was worth it.

Planning a group adventure

The best thing about going on an adventure with friends is that everyone brings their own skills and ideas, which makes your adventure amazing. But going on a group trip takes lots of planning so follow my group adventure guide below to plan your expedition.

Group adventure guide

Adventure pals: Who are the brave explorers you want to embark on this journey with? Your friends, siblings or maybe even your parents? Decide who you'd like to have by your side.

Destination: Where will your adventure take place? Will it be in your garden or at a nearby park? Or perhaps it'll be a virtual adventure from your own home. Choose a location that suits your idea.

◉ **Adventure essentials:** What will you need for your adventure? Think about the supplies and equipment that will make your adventure fun and safe, whether it's a map, snacks or a torch. Make sure to pack for all eventualities (take a look at my list of essentials on page 15 to get you started!).

◉ **Adventure challenges:** Plan some exciting challenges or activities to make your adventure unforgettable. Maybe it's finding hidden treasure, sharing stories or competing in virtual games. Get creative!

◉ **Safety first:** Don't forget about safety! If you're going outdoors, make sure you have the right gear. If it's a virtual adventure, set some rules to stay safe online.

Now, with your adventure plan in hand, you and your friends are all set to embark on a memorable journey. Get ready to create some awesome memories and explore like true adventurers!

Explorer's top tip

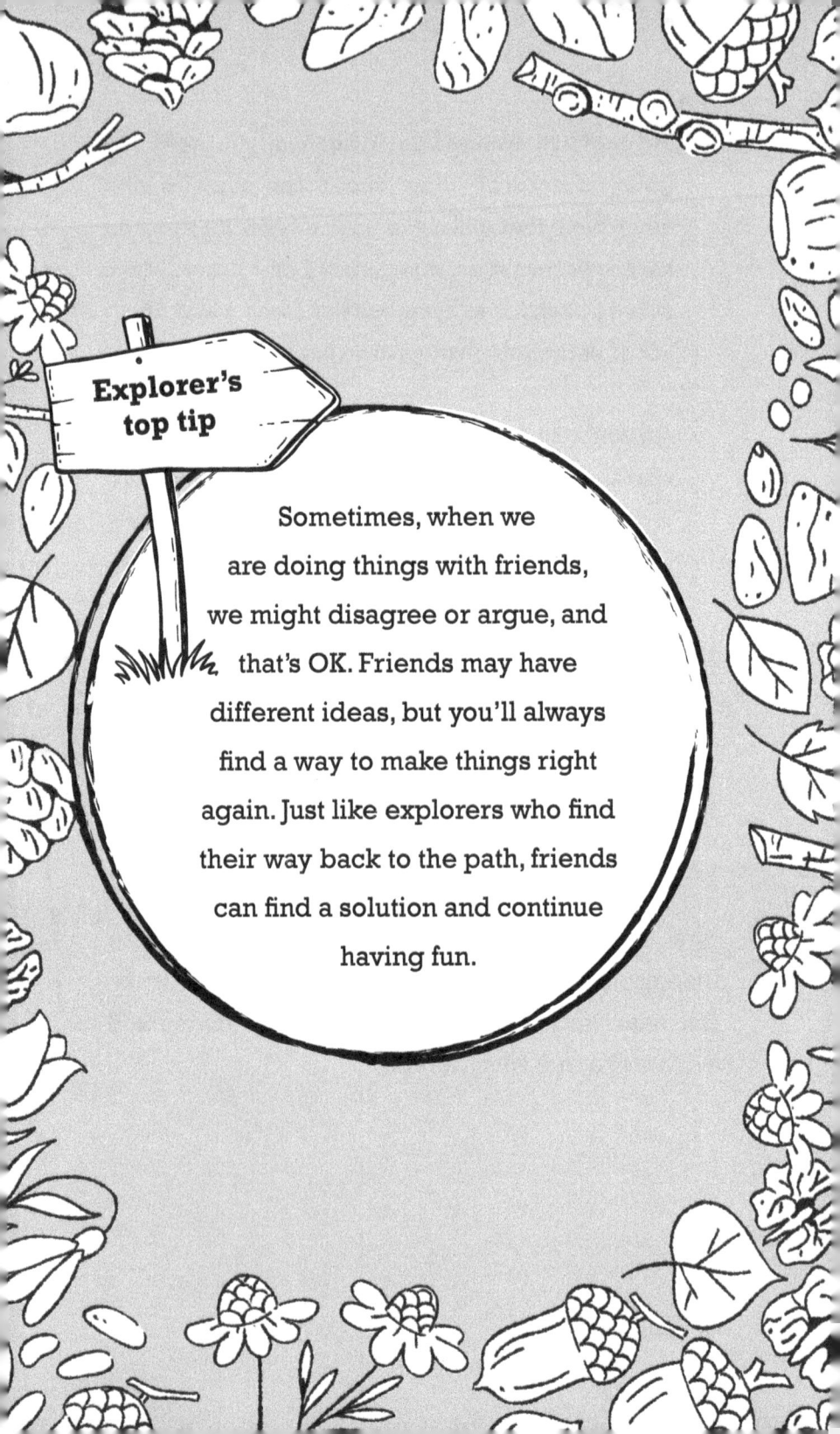

Sometimes, when we are doing things with friends, we might disagree or argue, and that's OK. Friends may have different ideas, but you'll always find a way to make things right again. Just like explorers who find their way back to the path, friends can find a solution and continue having fun.

Team step-up challenge

Why not compete with your friends to see who can do the most step-ups.

All you need is a step (it could be the bottom of your staircase) and a friend to compete with. Climb up and down the step one leg at a time as fast as you can for as long as you can. You can count together and cheer each other on. It's like climbing a mountain of fun, one step at a time!

How many step-ups did you do?

How many did your friends do?

Want to make it harder?
Why not try going up and down two steps at a time or hoping on and off one step. Just be careful that you don't go too fast, as you don't want to hurt yourself.

Distracting challenges

Try, try again! Remember how I tackled the midnight hours? Well, by morning I was still doing the same step-ups, encouraged by my friend who came to chat to me. It made it much easier! Sometimes, a little distraction can make a big difference. Just remember, even with distractions, counting your steps is key.

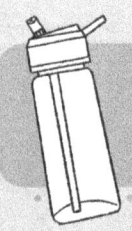

Why adventures with friends rock

Adventures with friends are the best kind – full of laughter, surprises and shared memories. Whether you're solving riddles, telling stories by the campfire or encouraging each other during challenges, being with friends makes every moment unforgettable.

Plus, when you face challenges together, they become a whole lot easier. Just like my 24-hour step-up challenge. It was tough, but having friends join me virtually gave me the strength to keep going. **When things get tough, friends become your superpower!** And remember, I'm also there with you each step of the way.

How to be a great team

Having a great adventure with your friends is super cool! But to make it even more awesome, here are my top ten tips for having a great group adventure:

1. Team talk: When you're on an adventure with your pals, make sure to keep talking to each other. This could be pointing out obstacles, asking for their help or sharing ideas.

2. Trust squad: Trust is the magic glue that holds your team together. When you trust your buddies, you can do daring stuff and try new things.

3. Mix it up: Your adventure team should be like a box of colourful crayons, not just one colour. Having friends with different talents and ideas makes problem-solving fun. You can come up with the most incredible solutions together!

4. Goal getters: Know what you want to achieve on your adventure and tell your friends. If you work together, you're more likely to achieve your goal.

5. Fun is key: Adventures are all about having a blast! So make sure you and your pals are having a great time. When everyone's happy, it makes the adventure even better.

6. Challenges are cool: Challenges will come up on your journey and that's OK. They help you learn how to work together.

7. Share the load: Don't go solo. Share tasks with your team so everyone can help; it makes it easier.

8. Cheer squad: Encourage your friends when things get tough. A high-five or a friendly word can make a big difference.

9. Patience pays: Like planting seeds and waiting for them to grow into big trees, building trust and becoming a good team takes time. So don't worry if everything isn't perfect right away. Keep having fun together!

10. Party time: When you achieve a goal on your adventure, throw a little celebration! Celebrate your victories with dance parties or tasty snacks.

Dream teams

Before you go off on your group adventure, be inspired by these teammates who, together, did remarkable things.

Space pioneers – Mae Jemison and the STS-47 astronaut crew: Mae Jemison and the crew of the STS-47 space mission embarked on extraordinary journeys into space where they carried out forty-four science experiments, furthering our understanding of space. Mae was the first African American woman to fly to space.

Environmental heroes – Isatou Ceesay and the recycling champions: Isatou Ceesay is an activist who started a recycling movement in her home country, The Gambia. But she didn't do it alone – she joined forces with other women in her community who helped recycle waste, clean up the streets and spoke up for a greener Earth. Together, they've made a big impact!

📍 **Mountaineering marvels – Sir Edmund Hillary and Tenzing Norgay:** These brave climbers were the first people to reach the top of the world's highest peak, Mount Everest. They faced icy challenges and high-altitude dangers, but proved that teamwork can overcome even the toughest mountains.

📍 **Ocean navigators – Ferdinand Magellan's crew:** Magellan and his crew were the first to sail around the world, proving that the Earth is round. Despite storms, hunger and rough seas, they completed a historic journey that expanded our understanding of the globe.

📍 **Polar pioneers – Roald Amundsen and his South Pole team:** Amundsen and his crew were the first to reach the South Pole. They faced freezing temperatures and treacherous conditions but worked together to survive the extreme environment.

Teamwork makes the dream work

When I went to Antarctica for my big adventure, I didn't do it all by myself; I needed help. I found people who had experience in those conditions and could offer me advice. **I had an amazing team of people who helped me every step of the way.** They helped me get ready for the icy cold by making sure I had all the right gear and nutritious food to eat, and they taught me how to stay safe. They were my adventure buddies and always happy to lend a hand.

I needed funding for the expedition and would email companies every single day to ask if they wanted to support me. But a lot of companies wouldn't respond, so it took me over a year and a half to get my first sponsor on board. But when I did, I was so glad I didn't give up trying! These incredible people helped me fund my Antarctic dream by funding the trip. Without them, I might have been stuck at home instead of going on this remarkable expedition.

So remember, even when you're off on your own adventures, there's always a team of amazing people cheering you on and wishing you the best. **Having a team to support you is the secret behind every successful explorer.**

CHAPTER NINE

SOLO EXPLORATION

Sometimes, the best companion for an adventure is . . . **you!** Being an explorer often means going on adventures by yourself. You might have a team supporting you, but they could be back at basecamp, a satellite phone call away, while you're out trekking in the wild. There's something so special about a solo adventure. It helps you get to know yourself better, find your strengths and discover your weaknesses, and you feel completely free. So let's learn how you can set out on a solo adventure in a safe way, or prepare for an adventure when you're older and discover the fantastic gift of spending time alone.

The wonder of being alone

The night before my first solo adventure, I felt a mixture of excitement and worry. I had to rely on just myself, and in doing so, I discovered that I had a lot more courage and independence than I realised. I was going on a hike in England, not too far away from home, but I still felt nervous because I didn't normally go alone. I usually had someone with me.

As I packed my backpack with all the essentials – a map, some snacks, a water bottle and a head torch – I couldn't help but wonder how the journey would go. The thought of exploring the woods and the winding trails all by myself was **both thrilling and a bit scary**.

That night, I checked the weather forecast and reviewed my map, making sure I knew the route well. I felt a bit like a superhero getting ready for an epic quest. Even though it wasn't an expedition to the furthest corners of the Earth, it was my own little adventure, and that made it special.

The next morning, as the sun rose, I set out on my hike. The familiar path seemed different – more mysterious and full of possibilities. The chirping birds and the rustling leaves in the gentle breeze became my companions. I felt a sense of freedom and empowerment I hadn't experienced before.

With every step, my confidence grew. I realised that I could navigate the trail, make decisions and solve small challenges all on my own. As I stood at the summit, gazing at the scenic view, I felt a deep sense of accomplishment. I had embraced the unknown, faced my fears and discovered a new side to myself.

Returning home that evening, I was tired but happy. My solo adventure had taught me that sometimes, stepping out of your comfort zone can lead to remarkable self-discovery. It was a reminder that even in familiar places, there are adventures waiting to unfold if you're willing to take that first step.

Preparing for your solo adventure

Before you begin your solo trip, you need to be fully prepared. This means doing careful research, packing all the important stuff and making sure someone you trust knows where you're going. **Safety always comes first.** Just like an experienced explorer, you've got to be extra thorough when getting ready.

Now, you're probably too young to have your first solo expedition in the great Sahara Desert or on the ice caps of the Arctic, but you could try pioneering somewhere a little closer to home, like your garden or your local park with a parent nearby. What could you explore there? Is there a pond full of frogspawn that you've been meaning to check out, or do you want to see how many laps of the garden or park you can do in five minutes?

Solo adventure challenge

Here's a cool challenge to get you started on your solo adventure. Pick a day when you can spend some time exploring, with a trusted adult nearby, and choose something to do. It could be a visit to a nearby nature spot, a trip to a quiet place in your local park or even camping all by yourself in your garden. Do you have somewhere in mind? Good – now grab a notebook and a pencil and fill a page in with your adventure by answering the questions below.

Before you go:

Draw a picture of the place you're having your solo adventure. How big is it? What trees and plants do you think you'll find there?

How long will it take you to get there and how will you get there?

What do you want to do when you get there?

On your adventure:

◎ Write down three things you see in your adventure spot.

◎ What kind of animals or plants can you find in your adventure location?

📍 Make up a fun song about your adventure. Why not sing it out loud too?!

📍 Are there other people here? Describe them.

📍 Take a moment to just listen. What sounds do you hear around you? Can you identify any bird calls, rustling leaves or distant voices?

Did you enjoy that your adventure? What was your favourite part?

Explorer's top tip

Famous explorer Amelia Earhart, who became the first woman to fly a plane across the Atlantic Ocean by herself, understood the power of solo exploration. She believed that being alone would help her find her hidden strengths and learn more about herself.

Facing challenges like a master explorer

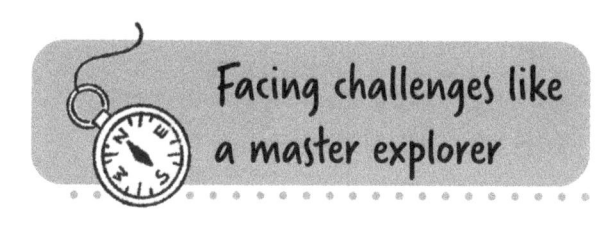

During your solo adventure, you will come across challenges you expect and challenges that surprise you. But no matter the challenge, you'll always find a way to overcome it. **Facing challenges alone can make you feel strong and brave.** It shows you how capable you are. Just like when I navigated through the trails during my solo adventure, you'll discover your own capabilities and face life's challenges with new-found courage. Each obstacle is a chance to prove you can handle anything that comes your way.

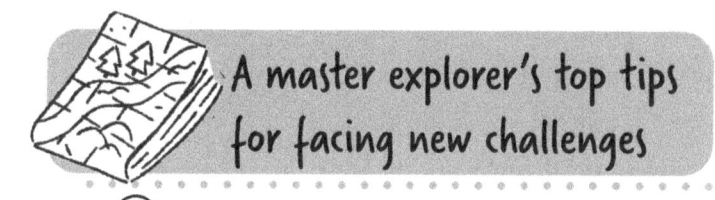

A master explorer's top tips for facing new challenges

Breaking problems into smaller steps: When you're faced with a big challenge, like getting lost, break it down into smaller, manageable steps. For example, stop, take a deep breath and look for familiar landmarks. If you're still unsure, don't hesitate to ask for help from a trusted adult. When

I was in Antarctica, I would take a small break every hour, and when I was finding it difficult, I would just think about that next hour. Sometimes I only concentrated on taking one step forward at a time.

Managing loneliness: Feeling alone during your adventure is natural. To overcome loneliness, try engaging with your surroundings. Observe the nature around you, make friends with local birds or start a nature journal to document your experience.

Dealing with fear: If you encounter something that scares you, remember that fear is a normal reaction. Take a moment to evaluate the situation. Is it a real danger or does it just feel scary because it's new? Trust your instincts, and if something doesn't feel right, it's OK to leave and seek help.

Navigating without getting lost: Learning basic navigation skills, like reading maps, following trails and understanding landmarks, can help you stay on the right track. If you do get lost, don't panic. Retrace your steps or use your map to guide you back.

📍 **Handling unpredictable weather:** Weather can change quickly and being prepared is key. Check the forecast before your adventure and pack accordingly. Always bring extra layers, a rain jacket and sun protection, no matter the weather when you start.

📍 **Finding food and water:** If you're out for a while, you might need a snack or water. Plan ahead by bringing a small supply of snacks like energy bars, nuts or fruit and a reusable water bottle. Foraging for edible plants can be fun and educational, but make sure to learn which plants are safe to eat first.

📍 **Dealing with minor injuries:** Accidents happen, but most can be handled with a basic first aid kit. Pack essentials like plasters, antiseptic wipes and a small bandage. Learn some first aid basics, like how to clean a wound or stop minor bleeding.

📍 **Making safe decisions:** If you ever feel unsure about something, it's perfectly fine to pause and make safe decisions. Your safety should always be a top priority. Don't take unnecessary risks and don't be afraid to call for help if you need it.

Exploring solo is a wonderful way to discover your inner strength and resourcefulness. Remember that it's OK to face challenges, and each one is a valuable lesson in your adventurous journey. Stay curious, be prepared and trust yourself – you've got this!

The gift of discovering you

At the heart of a solo adventure is the **incredible gift of discovering yourself.** You can use your time alone to think about your dreams, goals and even your worries. You can learn to trust your feelings, make decisions on your own and enjoy your own company. Going on solo adventures can make you grow as an adventurer and as a person.

As you set out on your solo adventures, remember that **being alone doesn't mean being lonely.** It's a chance to become more independent. So, my brave solo explorers, open your hearts to the world of solo exploration and you'll find endless possibilities inside yourself.

CHAPTER TEN
WHERE TO GO ON YOUR NEXT ADVENTURE

Hey, explorer! Ready to turn your expedition dreams into a reality? Then let's pick a destination. Perhaps you want to try out a new park, or maybe you're going to the beach or up a mountain. Wherever you're going, get ready to learn how to kick-start your journey.

Why I chose to explore Antarctica

When I was a kid, I didn't know a lot about Antarctica, just that it was very far away and very cold. As I grew up, I knew I wanted to do a big challenge to show that I could achieve anything. When somebody mentioned Antarctica to me, I decided to learn more by looking up information online. I started with a simple search – 'How do you get to Antarctica'.

Throughout my life, I've encountered people who doubted me. They said I wasn't smart enough for university, but I was, and I even got my master's degree. They said I couldn't join the Army, but I did, and I made a career out of it. Some people said I couldn't do things because of my background and my gender. I'm British Indian. I was born in England but have family roots in India, and sometimes when people don't know many people from your background, they put you into stereotypes. **Stereotypes are when people mistakenly believe something about a person or thing based on how they look from the outside.** Sometimes these stereotypes came from people outside of my community but also from inside. Their words frustrated me, but they also fuelled my determination to prove them wrong.

I stopped listening to the people that told me I couldn't, and I decided to embark on **an extraordinary adventure to prove that I could.** Antarctica became my goal, a place where I could show that anyone, regardless of their background or gender, could achieve incredible things.

Have you ever heard the saying, 'It's not where you're from, it's where you're going'? Well, that's a saying I live by. I wanted to show that it doesn't matter where we come from or what we look like – we can all achieve our dreams. And you know what's even cooler? You don't have to know everything at the start. We all start somewhere, even if it's just with a curious online search.

Taking the first step

Researching Antarctica online was the first step to my expedition there. What will be the first step for your adventure? Perhaps it's deciding what kind of adventure you want to have. Will it be indoors or outdoors? Will you be going with friends or family? Do you want to walk, ride your bike or scoot?

Sometimes the first step can be the trickiest. I was worried when I first chose to go to Antarctica. Some people even said I couldn't be a polar explorer. But you know what? I went anyway. I knew I wanted to inspire others, and that helped me believe in myself even when things felt tough.

Destination unknown

Still not sure where to go on your first big trip, or perhaps you want help deciding where to go next? Choose an answer to each of these questions and then add up how many times you choose answer A, B and C. Whichever one you choose the most will help you find your next adventure destination.

Your answers might lead you to the park, the woods or somewhere more exotic!

Question 1: What type of nature do you find most appealing?
A) I enjoy nature, but close to home is where it's at!
B) I like nature, especially in local parks
C) Exotic and distant nature adventures are what excite me!

Question 2: How much space do you prefer for your adventures?
A) I prefer wide, open spaces near my doorstep
B) Local parks and woods with open areas are just right
C) I'm all about exploring vast, distant lands

Question 3: What kind of wildlife excites you the most?
A) Birds, squirrels and local critters
B) Ducks, frogs and familiar animals
C) Lions, tigers and exotic creatures

Question 4: How do you like to spend your weekends?
A) Exploring my garden and nearby nature
B) Visiting local parks and nature reserves
C) Planning adventures abroad

Question 5: What type of scenery appeals to you?
A) A mixture of greenery and buildings – I like seeing lots of people
B) Local parks, rivers and trees
C) Uncharted forests, mountains or sandy dunes

Question 6: How far would you go for a fun adventure?
A) Just outside my door
B) A short drive, cycle or walk
C) Anywhere around the world

Results:

Mostly As: The Doorstep Discoverer!
You find endless wonder right outside your door. Your own garden or local neighbourhood is a treasure trove of exploration. There's a whole world to discover just a step away from home.

Mostly Bs: The Local Adventurer!
You appreciate the beauty of nearby parks and the charm of your local woods. Nature close to home, with open areas and friendly ducks, frogs and other familiar animals, is your go-to playground. Get set for thrilling expeditions, whether it's a short drive, cycle or walk away!

Mostly Cs: The Exotic Explorer!
Exotic destinations and thrilling adventures in far-off lands are your calling. Whether it's exploring the jungles of Southeast Asia or experiencing the African savannah, your next journey awaits in a distant paradise. Time to start planning your global adventure with your family!

Breaking boundaries

The world is full of explorers, thinkers and dreamers of all kinds. And guess what? They don't all look the same. When I first said I was going to be a polar explorer, some people thought that was strange. They thought I didn't look like a polar explorer. Can you believe it? Yes, I didn't have the long beard and I wasn't a white man like in the pictures in history books, but that didn't mean I couldn't be an explorer. Polar explorers can look like anyone and everyone – including you!

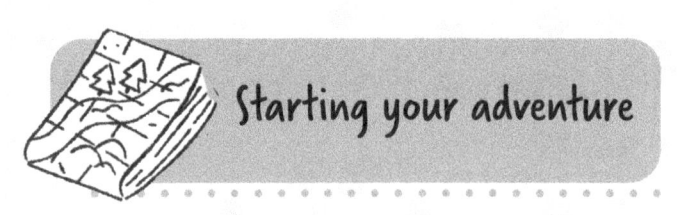

Starting your adventure

Starting something new might feel a bit scary, but you're not alone. I felt unsure when I first landed in Antarctica. I was about to take on this big, scary expedition and it felt daunting. But I reminded myself why I was doing it – **to push myself and show everyone that explorers don't all have beards** – and that helped me believe I could do it.

Believing in yourself is the key. Think about why you want to do it. When you believe, you're halfway there!

Chart your adventure course

Now you've taken the quiz and decided where to explore, it's time to plan your journey. We know that the best explorers are always prepared and that's because they have a plan.

Follow these steps to plan your ultimate adventure. Write down your answers in a notebook.

Step one: Think of something you'd love to try. It can be as exciting as exploring a forest or as simple as splashing in puddles!

I want to ...

Step two: Where can you do this?

I can do this ...

Step three: What do you need to wear? For example, if you're exploring in the rain, you'll need a raincoat and wellies.

I am going to wear . . .

Step four: How will you get there? Do you need your parents to drive you there or can you walk or cycle?

I'll get there by . . .

Step five: What will you do there? Are you just splashing in puddles or are you on the hunt for butterflies too?

I am going to . . .

Step six: How will you get home? The same way you got there, or is there another adventure you could have on the way home?

I will get home by ...

Congratulations! You've charted a course for adventure! You're all set for your next unforgettable journey. Whether it's a tiny step or a giant leap, remember that every explorer starts with curiosity and a dream. Your adventure is waiting – embrace the unknown, have fun and believe in your limitless potential.

The adventure is calling — are you ready?

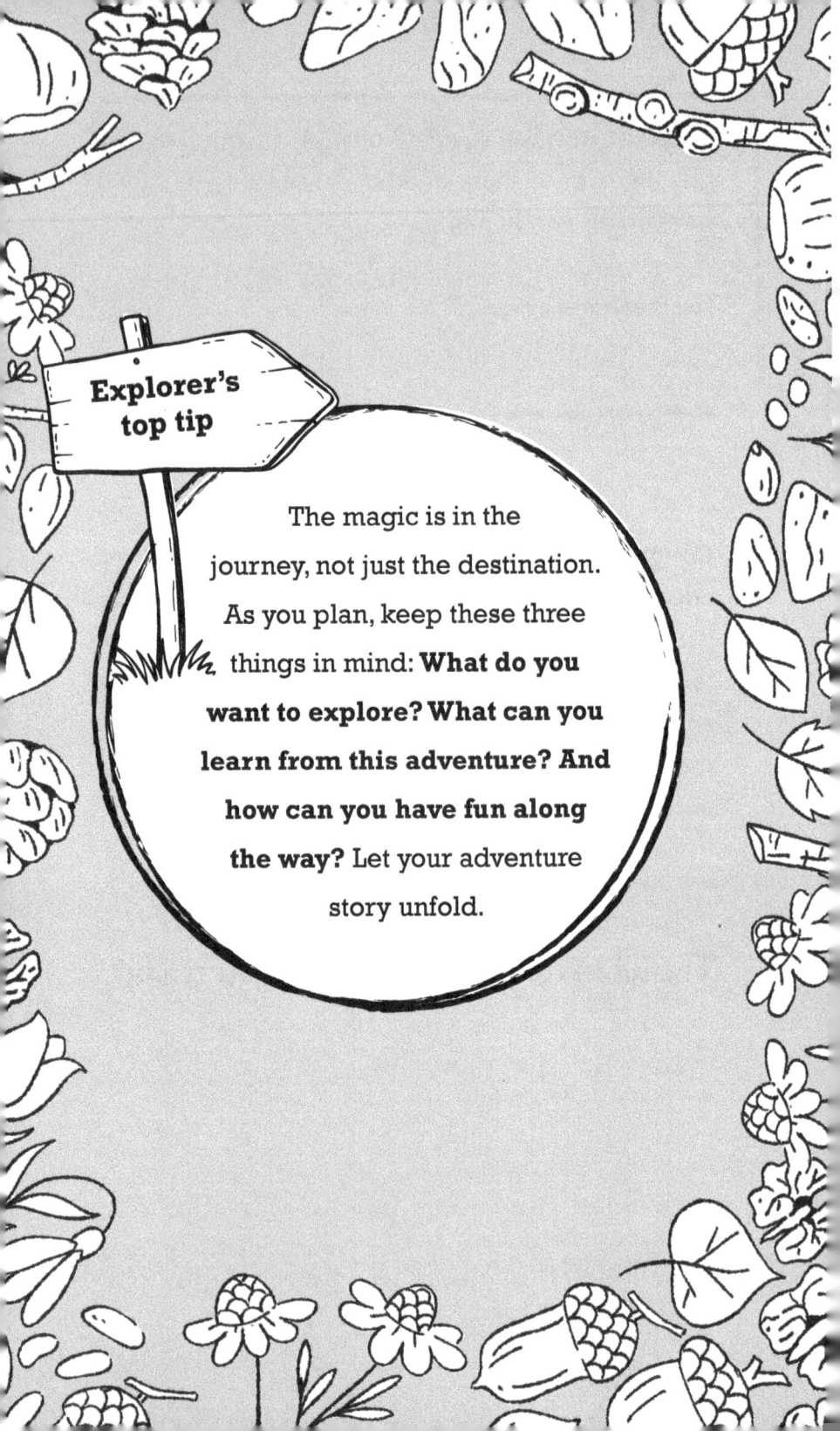

Explorer's top tip

The magic is in the journey, not just the destination. As you plan, keep these three things in mind: **What do you want to explore? What can you learn from this adventure? And how can you have fun along the way?** Let your adventure story unfold.

Diving into the unknown

It can be scary visiting a new place. Trying new things might feel like entering a forest for the first time; you're uncertain about what you'll find inside, but once you venture in, it becomes an exciting journey. And you're not alone. You're armed with curiosity, courage and the belief that you can achieve anything you set your mind to. It's OK to be a bit scared, but don't let that stop you.

Your adventure planning checklist

It's time to get out there and make memories – but if you ever need guidance or motivation, remember my top tips for having adventures.

Dream big: Whether you want to go on a trek to the South Pole or dig around your own garden, the possibilities are endless!

You look just like an explorer: Remember, you don't have to look a certain way or be a certain person to be an explorer. You're already one.

- **Stay curious:** Curiosity opens up so many possibilities. Find the answer to that question and see what's round that corner. Exciting things await.

- **It's OK to be scared:** A little fear can help us keep safe, but if there's no danger, push away your fears and prove to yourself that you can get through it.

- **Believe in yourself:** You can do this, and you might inspire others too.

- **Take the leap:** The first step might be tricky but it's the start of an incredible adventure. Dive in!

You're already an adventure expert

Guess what? You're already a pro at trying new things. You're reading this book, after all! When I first started exploring, I didn't know much, but I kept learning, I kept making mistakes and, ultimately, I became a better explorer for it. **Everyone has to start somewhere and you're already halfway there!**

CHAPTER ELEVEN

MAKING DO WITH WHAT YOU HAVE

No explorer is perfect, and sometimes we mess up. We might forget to bring a piece of equipment, accidentally rip our map in two or simply lose our torch. These things happen, and when they do, **it's important not to panic**. There's always a solution to any problem we come across; we just need to take the time to think about what it could be. Thankfully, I've made lots of mistakes and worked out lot of solutions, so I can teach you how to make do with what you already have.

The case of the forgotten loo roll

I've got a funny story to tell you about a big mistake I made, and it involves something we all use every day – toilet paper! **Yep, explorers need to bring loo roll on expeditions**, and sometimes we're not very good at packing it!

I felt really prepared for my epic trip to Antarctica. I had checked every piece of my kit and equipment and was ready to go. The trip didn't have the best start. My flight to Antarctica from Chile was delayed by a week as the weather was bad. By the time we reached Antarctica, I was eager to start and asked to begin the very next day. **I didn't want to wait any longer!** I had everything planned out, even down to the number of tissues I'd need for each day. Smart, right?

I had packed the first ten days' worth of toilet paper in my top left pocket. But here comes the twist – on day eleven, I searched my sled for the rest of the toilet paper, but it wasn't there. I started to panic. I could feel the wind getting stronger and stronger. I couldn't spend the entire day searching for it! Once I'd checked the front three bags, my heart sank. I couldn't believe **I had forgotten the rest of the loo roll**.

Now, being the determined explorer I am, I didn't let this setback stop me. For the next thirty days of my trip, I used snow as makeshift toilet paper. It was quite a chilly solution, but it worked! Then, after thirty days of using snow as toilet paper, I went into my last food bag, at the back of my sled, and guess what I found? My precious toilet paper stash! It was like finding treasure and I treated it as a luxury for the rest of my journey.

Here's the thing, we all mess up from time to time. It can be frustrating, sure, but it's also a chance to learn and grow. Looking back, I realised I could've done a few things differently to avoid my funny toilet paper mishap. I could have spent another few hours in Antarctica before starting my journey instead of rushing. I could have packed better or written a list of where everything was kept.

But instead of dwelling on it, **I turned it into a funny memory**.

Alternative solutions

You're halfway up a mountain and you realise that you've remembered your reusable water bottle but forgotten to put any water in it. What do you do? Luckily for you, I have made this very mistake – and others – so here are a few easy alternatives for when you've forgotten some of your kit, and some tips to help avoid these problems in the first place.

What to do when...

Problem 1: You're out of water

◉ Look for a sparkling stream or river, but be sure to ask an adult if it's OK to drink from it.

◉ Search for juicy berries or coconuts to munch on. But first check with an adult to make sure they're safe to eat.

◉ If you're near home or a friend's house, ask for a sip of water.

Problem 2: Your socks get soaked

- Take off those soggy socks and give them a good squeeze.
- Lay your socks in a sunny spot to dry.
- If possible, have a spare pair of dry socks to change into.
- Take advantage of breaks to let your feet air out and dry naturally.

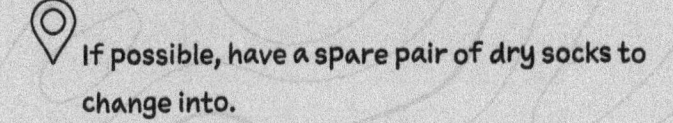

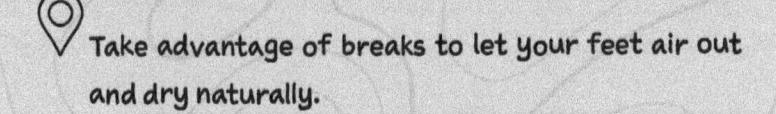

Problem 3: Your torch stops working

- In the daytime, let the sunshine guide your way.
- Always carry extra batteries or a spare torch.
- Buy a wind-up torch. You just wind the battery to get it to work. No need for batteries.

Problem 4: You forgot your comfy sleeping bag

- Layer up! Put on extra clothes to keep warm.
- Find some leaves, grass or pine needles to rest on; it's like a natural mattress.
- Snuggle up with a friend to share warmth if you're not alone.

Problem 5: Your shoelaces keep coming untied

- Tie them in a double knot — it's like a super knot that stays put.
- Look for elastic shoelaces — they stretch, so they're less likely to untie.
- If all else fails, ask a friend or an adult to help you with those tricky laces.

Problem 6: Your backpack zipper gets stuck

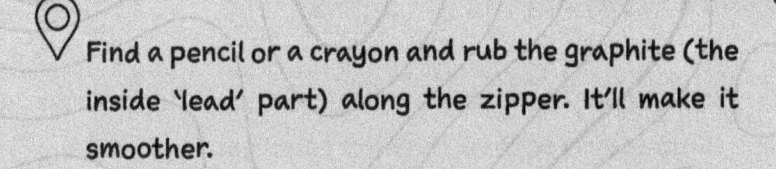

⦿ Find a pencil or a crayon and rub the graphite (the inside 'lead' part) along the zipper. It'll make it smoother.

⦿ If you have a bar of soap, rub it on the zipper to make it glide more easily.

⦿ Ask a friend or a grown-up to help you unstick it.

Problem 7: You get blisters on your feet

⦿ Start with comfy, well-fitting shoes to prevent blisters.

⦿ If you feel a hot spot on your foot, stop and put a bandage or special padded tape on it to avoid a full-blown blister.

⦿ In you get a blister, keep it clean and cover it with a bandage. Give your feet a break too.

Problem 8: You forgot your sunglasses on a sunny day

- Use your hand as a makeshift visor, holding it above your eyes to block the direct sunlight.

- Find some natural shade like a big rock or a tree and take breaks in the shade.

- If you have a hat, wear it to shield your eyes from the sun.

Problem 9: You get lost on a hike

- Stay calm and don't wander too far; try to retrace your steps.

- Carry a whistle to signal for help — three short blasts, then pause and repeat.

- If you have a phone or a compass, use them to help you find your way back.

> **Problem 10: It starts raining, and you forgot your raincoat**
>
> 📍 Look for shelter, like a tree or a cave, where you can wait for the rain to stop.
>
> 📍 Use big leaves as a makeshift rain hat to keep your head dry.
>
> 📍 Remember, a little rain can make an adventure even more fun!

Let your imagination run wild! Big leaves make great plates, and small leaves can become your tools.

Use a stick to carve a mini fork or spoon – just ask a grown-up to help.

Go ahead and eat with your hands, but remember to wash them first if you've been on a wild adventure.

These clever tricks will turn your adventure into an exciting and memorable journey. **Just remember, explorers like you are great at finding solutions.**

It's OK to forget things

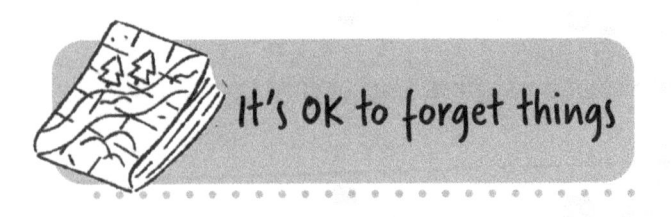

When you make mistakes, it's important to take a step back and see what you can learn from them, but you don't need to dwell on them. It's totally OK to forget some of your equipment before your adventure. **Life's all about learning, growing and finding humour in the unexpected.** Maybe you'll find a better way to pack your backpack next time; perhaps having to use an alternative solution will become a whole new adventure. Sometimes your mistakes might just turn into the best stories ever! Keep smiling and feel free to laugh at yourself when you mess up.

Can you fix it?

Test your knowledge on fixing your mistakes by answering these questions.

Question 1: You're out exploring when you realise your jacket has a tear in it. How can you fix it?

Question 2: Your hat blows away and lands in a puddle of mud. How can you clean it?

Question 3: Oops! You've lost one of your gloves on a cold day. What's the quickest way to keep your hand warm?

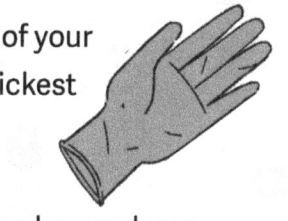

Question 4: Your shoelaces have broken and you can't tie your shoes. What can you do?

Question 5: You find a big stick that you want to keep, but it's too long for your backpack. How can you carry it with you?

Question 6: Your favourite adventure toy or tool breaks. What's an easy way to fix it?

Question 7: You drop your sunglasses and one of the lenses falls out. What's the quickest way to fix them?

Question 8: Your torch stops working and you're in the dark. What's a simple solution?

Find the answers on page 186.

Explorer's top tip

Here's a tip for all you budding adventurers out there. Make a checklist before every big trip. List all the things you'll need, from toilet paper to snacks and maps. And don't forget to double-check it! It will help you avoid funny mishaps.

Laugh it off

When you mess up, it can be hard to forgive yourself. That's why I decided that I was always going to laugh at my mistakes instead of getting frustrated or upset. **Laughter can make you feel awesome**, and when you laugh, all sorts of amazing things happen to your body and your heart.

CHAPTER TWELVE

GO WILD WITH NATURE CRAFTS

Now you know how to make do with things you might find in the wild, it's time to learn how to be creative with the wonders of nature. **Nature is a giant art store**, full of treasures waiting for you to craft them into amazing creations. Let's jump into the world of nature crafts and let our inner artists shine!

Keeping busy with crafts

On one of my adventures with my niece, Simran, we went on a walk through the woods and it felt like a magical world. There were big trees, all sorts of plants and the sounds of birds and insects going about their days. It was amazing! I wanted to remember this day with Simran, so we decided to do some nature crafts together.

We started by going on a little adventure in the woods. **Our mission?** To find leaves, twigs and colourful flowers to use for our crafts. Simran was so curious and excited. We found leaves of all shapes and colours and wildflowers that looked like tiny pieces of art.

We then arranged the leaves, twigs and flowers on a piece of paper. We did leaf rubbings, which turned the leaves' hidden patterns into beautiful art on our pages. While we created our nature crafts, we talked about the animals and insects living in the forest and how important it is to take care of nature. It was so much fun and we both got to learn about the magic of the great outdoors.

The beauty of nature crafts

Nature crafts are a fantastic way to have fun outdoors while making beautiful things. Whether you're in a lush forest, by the beach or even just in your garden, there's inspiration all around you. Plus, crafting with nature is not only fun but also good for the Earth.

Go wild

There are so many fun things you can make with everyday items you'll find in nature. But before you can make anything, you need to gather supplies from Mother Nature's store. Can you find all of these?

- **Leaves:** Collect colourful leaves of all shapes and sizes as these are great decorations.

- **Sticks and twigs:** Find straight sticks or twisty twigs for building structures.

- **Pine cones:** These are a perfect base for loads of craft projects.

- **Stones and pebbles:** Look for smooth, flat stones and cool-shaped pebbles.

- **Flowers:** Colourful flowers bring beauty to any craft, and they smell great too.

- **Acorns, chestnuts and seeds:** These are awesome for decorating and adding texture.

Now let's make an exciting craft project: **a leaf lantern.**

Materials you'll need:

- Leaves
- A glass jar (like an empty jam or pasta sauce jar)
- PVA glue
- A paintbrush
- A tea light candle

How to make a leaf lantern

1. Go on a leaf-collecting adventure. Ask an adult to go with you and together, choose some beautiful leaves with interesting shapes and colours.

2. Gently wash the leaves and let them dry out completely. Make sure they are flat and not too crinkled.

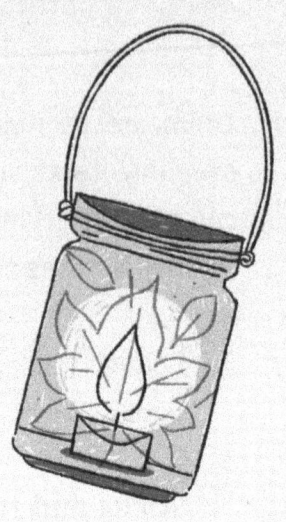

3. While the leaves are drying, wash and dry the glass jar. It should be clean and free from any labels or sticky residue.

4. When the leaves and jar are ready, take your paintbrush and apply a thin layer of PVA glue to the outside of the jar. Make sure the glue covers the jar evenly.

5. Carefully place your colourful leaves on the jar's surface. You can arrange them in any pattern you like. Maybe you want to create a special design or copy one you've seen in a magazine.

6. Once your leaves are in position, apply another layer of glue on top of the leaves. This will help seal them in place.

7. Give your leaf-covered jar some time to dry. It might take a few hours or even days.

8. Once your leaf lantern is dry, put a tea light candle inside the jar. Be sure to ask an adult for help when lighting the candle.

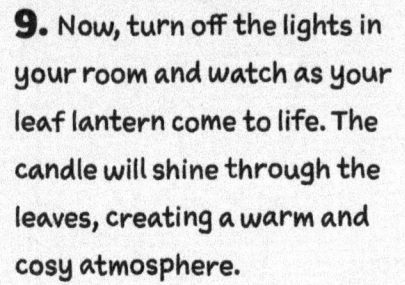

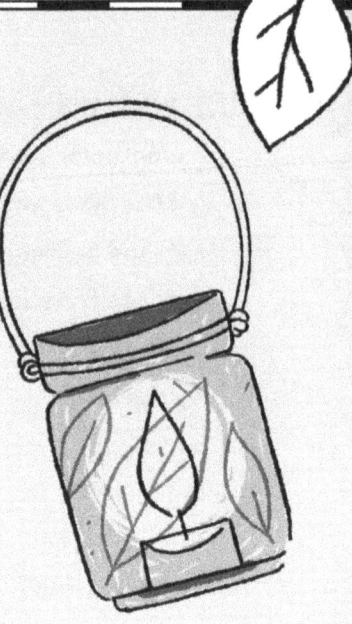

9. Now, turn off the lights in your room and watch as your leaf lantern come to life. The candle will shine through the leaves, creating a warm and cosy atmosphere.

These leaf lanterns are a wonderful way to celebrate the beauty of nature and make your home feel extra special. Just remember to be safe around candles and never leave them unattended. Enjoy the magical glow of your DIY Leaf Luminaries!

Getting crafty

There are so many other nature crafts you can do. Why not try one of these?

Story stones: Grab some smooth rocks and paint pictures or symbols on them to make story stones. Each stone can stand for a character, an object or an idea.

Leaf art: Arrange leaves in different patterns or glue them on to paper to make leafy art.

Nature bunting: Use string to hang things like sticks, leaves and pine cones from a branch to create bunting for your room.

Twig picture frames: Make rustic frames for your favourite outdoor photos using twigs.

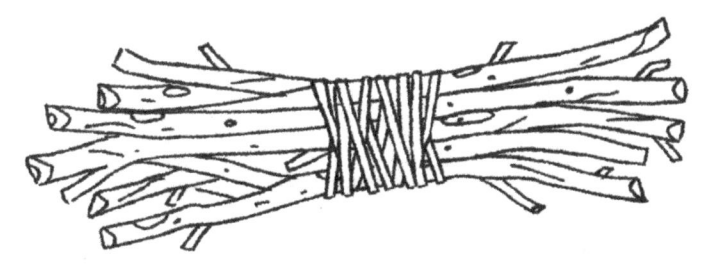

📍 **Flower crowns:** Weave delicate flowers or petals into a crown fit for a nature king or queen.

📍 **Leaf pressing:** Keep leaves safe between paper and heavy books to flatten them. You can then use them to decorate other things, like a bookmark (you could even use it for this book!).

Explorer's top tip

Always remember to be kind to nature while collecting materials. Take only what you need and leave the environment just as beautiful as you found it. That way, others can enjoy the same beauty you did.

Sharing your nature crafts

One of the best things about nature crafts is sharing them with others. You can give your creations as gifts to family, friends or teachers to spread the joy of nature's art. Crafting with friends can be loads of fun too! Why not invite your fellow explorers on a hunt for nature's goodies and then make each other presents out of them. The perfect memento from an adventure.

The wonder of nature

There's nothing an adventurer loves more than being outdoors, and making nature crafts is a fun way to blend your love for the outdoors with your creative spirit. When you create these treasures, not only do you make beautiful things, but you will also feel more connected to the natural world. **It helps you appreciate the natural resources the Earth provides** and it's a good reminder of just how precious and important it is to protect it. So, young artists, grab your supplies, head outside and let nature be your guide. Happy crafting!

CHAPTER THIRTEEN

NIGHT-TIME MAGIC

Have you ever been on an adventure in the dark? Well, master explorer, it's time you learned all about the amazing adventures you can have when the stars come out. Night-time turns the world into a mysterious place full of secrets just waiting for you to find. Grab your torch, put on your outdoor clothes and let's dive into the **enchantment of night-time adventures**!

Whispers in the dark

Night-time adventures with the Army were always quite exciting. On these exercises, we had to rely on our other **four senses (taste, smell, sound and touch)** because we weren't allowed to use our head torches to see where we were going.. We needed to learn to navigate the terrain in the dark in case we didn't have torches in the future.

As my eyes slowly adjusted to the darkness, the world around me began to reveal itself. I could make out the silhouettes of my teammates, their dark figures moving stealthily through the night. **We communicated through quiet whispers and hand signals, our gestures saying more than words ever could.**

The sounds of the night became our companions. I listened to the wind whispering through the trees, creating a gentle, eerie melody. **It felt like the forest was sharing its secrets with us.** And while we were as silent as the night, I could still hear the soft, rhythmic steps of my team, reassuring me that I wasn't alone.

Sometimes, we'd come across animals like owls, hooting, or distant foxes, calling to one another. It was a reminder that **nature never sleeps** and there's a world of activity in the darkness if you pay attention.

These night-time adventures taught me **the value of patience, observation and teamwork.** It was incredible how my senses became sharper in the absence of light and those experiences were both challenging and unforgettable.

The world at night

When we're usually tucked up in bed sleeping, the night comes alive with magic. Creatures like owls, foxes and fireflies wake up and start their routines. Night-time adventures are your chance to meet these fascinating creatures and uncover their secrets.

Which of these nocturnal animals have you already seen in the wild?

- Hedgehogs
- Foxes
- Bats
- Mice
- Moths
- Badgers
- Moles
- Toads
- Otters
- Owls

Getting ready for a night adventure

It's dark outside but you're not in bed. You're getting ready to go on a night-time expedition with a trusted grown-up and maybe a cuddly toy for reassurance. You're going to see and hear lots of new and exciting animals. But before you set off on your quest, a little preparation is important. Gather up all these things from around your home.

A torch: Your trusty torch to brighten up the darkness and reveal the hidden wonders of the night.

Outdoor clothes: You want to make sure you're warm enough while you're out exploring.

Trainers: Comfortable shoes for your walk.

Binoculars: Perfect for spotting flying night-dwellers.

A blanket: To lie on when you're stargazing.

A flask (if you have one): With a hot chocolate or your favourite hot drink to keep you warm.

Starry skies story time

Well done, brave explorer. You've made it outside. Find a good spot to place your blanket and lie down on top of it to gaze up at the night sky. Can you spot any constellations or shooting stars? Here are some common constellations to look out for...

Orion: Known as 'The Hunter', Orion is one of the most recognisable constellations with its distinctive three-star belt.

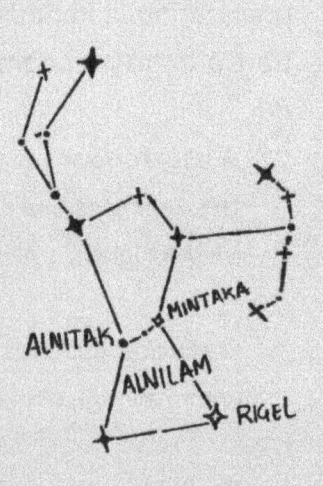

Ursa Major: The 'Big Dipper' is part of the Ursa Major constellation and resembles a large ladle or spoon.

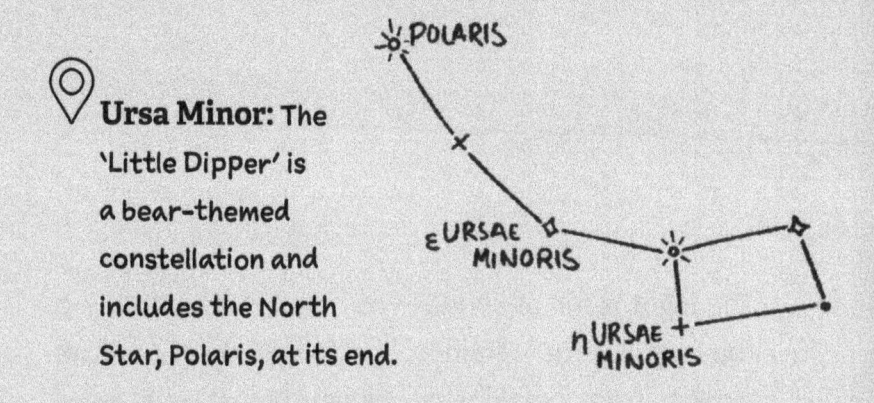

📍 **Ursa Minor:** The 'Little Dipper' is a bear-themed constellation and includes the North Star, Polaris, at its end.

```
         ☀ POLARIS
          ·
           ·
            × 
             ·
              ·
   ε URSAE ◇‧‧‧‧‧‧‧‧‧‧‧☀‧‧‧‧‧‧‧‧‧◇
     MINORIS            ·          ·
                        ·          ·
                    η URSAE +‧‧‧‧‧‧‧●
                      MINORIS
```

While you're stargazing, see if any stories come to mind. There's nothing better than telling your fellow stargazer a story or two. **Let your imagination run wild!**

When I was a kid, I used to visit family in India, and one of the things I loved the most was sleeping on a menjha outside, under the open sky. A menjha is a comfy bed that's set up outdoors. Imagine a big, sturdy net or cot made from ropes or fabric, sort of like a hammock but wider. It's a wonderful place to relax and enjoy the fresh air. In India, I often used them to sleep or just hang out under the open sky. It's perfect for gazing at the stars, telling stories or taking a cosy nap.

On the nights I would lie under the stars as a kid, my family would often join me and share the most incredible stories! It made night-time adventures so much fun.

Listen

The night is full of sounds you might not hear during the day. Listen carefully. You might hear crickets singing, frogs croaking or the gentle rustle of leaves in the breeze. These sounds are the night's special language, and by paying attention you can understand their messages.

For example, if you hear lots of leaves crunching, it might mean an animal is running or moving nearby. If you hear a chorus of frogs, it could be a sign that there's water or a pond close by.
These night-time sounds are nature's way of telling you what's happening in the dark. So **keep your ears open and learn to speak the language of the night!**

Explorer's top tip

Did you know that fireflies talk to each other using flashes of light? It's their own secret code for chatting in the dark. Try to spot these magical insects during your night-time adventure.

Animal spotting

With your trusty torch, take a look around. What can you see? Was that the flash of a tail or the whites of a nosy animal's eyes? **Don't be scared – these animals don't want to hurt you.** They're probably more afraid of you then you are of them. Just to be safe, follow my top tips for being kind to nocturnal animals.

Tips for not disturbing wildlife

📍 **Be quiet:** Keep your voice down and avoid making loud noises. Animals are sensitive to sound, and sudden loud noises can startle them.

📍 **Use a red light:** If you have a torch with a red light setting, use that instead of a bright white light. Red light is less likely to disturb animals' natural behaviour.

📍 **Don't shine light in their eyes:** Avoid shining your torch directly into an animal's eyes. It can temporarily blind them and cause distress.

📍 **Keep a safe distance:** Don't approach animals too closely. Use binoculars or the zoom function on your camera to get a better look without getting too close.

📍 **Stay still:** When you spot an animal, try to stay as still as possible. Sudden movements can frighten them away.

📍 **Respect their space:** Remember that you're a guest in their habitat. Keep a safe distance and avoid disturbing their nests or homes.

📍 **Clean up after yourself:** If you've brought snacks or food, make sure to clean up all your litter. Leaving rubbish behind can harm animals and their environment.

📍 **Learn about local wildlife:** Take the time to learn about the animals that live in the area you're exploring. Knowing more about them can help you understand their behaviour and needs.

By following these tips, you can enjoy your nocturnal adventures while being respectful and considerate of the animals that share the night with you.

Soak in the magic

One of the most amazing things about night-time adventures is how **calm and peaceful everything becomes**. The busy daytime world takes a rest, the parks are empty and most of the world goes to sleep. This time is magical. **Let the nocturnal animals show you their secret world**; gaze up at the constellations and tell stories about them and breathe deeply. **This moment is just for you.**

Now the night has shown you its secrets, you'll look at nature in a completely different way when daylight comes. That tree won't just be your climbing tree – it's the owl's home. That pond won't just have fish in it – toads live there too. Enjoy your night-time adventure.

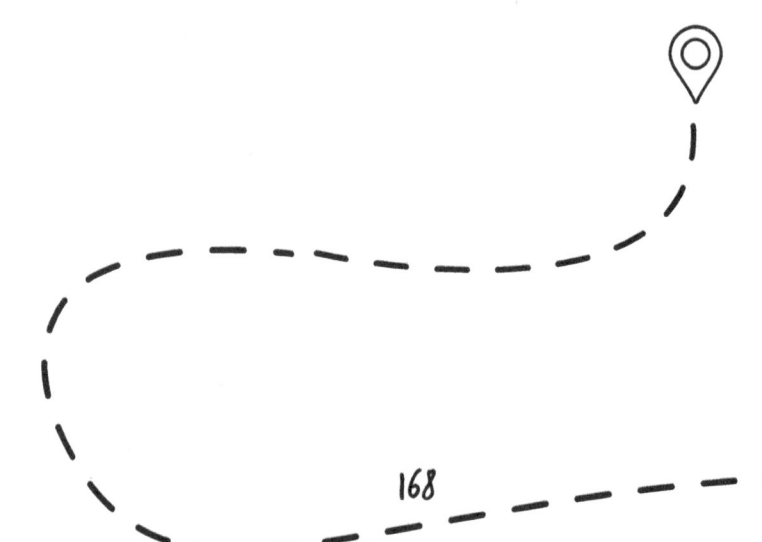

CHAPTER FOURTEEN

EMBRACE YOUR INNER EXPLORER

It can be hard to stay motivated when you're on your adventures. Being an explorer is thrilling, but sometimes the journey can be tough, you can feel lonely and you might just feel, well, rubbish. That's OK. Every explorer finds it hard to keep going at times, especially when it feels like no one is in your corner. That's why we must become **resilient and be our own cheerleaders**. Let's discover how to become our own most enthusiastic supporters and embrace our inner explorers.

Tired of tyre training

To prepare for the challenging task of pulling a sled with all my gear across Antarctica, I started dragging tyres around. It sounds like a unique training idea, but it is quite common for polar explorers. At first, it felt a bit strange, because people in the local parks would often stop and stare at what I was doing. **I couldn't help but feel a bit self-conscious** because it seemed like everyone's eyes were on me.

But then something magical happened. Some curious people approached me and asked what I was training for. When I shared the exciting details of my upcoming adventure, they thought it was **super cool**! It made me realise that what I was doing wasn't just about getting in shape; it was about inspiring others.

I continued my tyre training, and over time, I stopped worrying about what people might think. I knew that the unique and unconventional method was helping me build the strength and endurance I needed for my Antarctic journey.

In fact, I even brought those trusty tyres with me when I visited schools to talk about my adventures with students. I introduced them to my training buddies, tyre 1 and tyre 2. These tyres became quite the celebrities in the classroom and students loved getting involved and trying their hand at tyre dragging. It was a fun way to show them that preparing for an adventure can be both creative and inspiring. Tyre 1 and tyre 2 were always up for the challenge and they never missed a chance to be part of the action!

Understanding unkindness

When people aren't so kind, it's often because they're **feeling unsure or worried about themselves**. They might even be **jealous of how brave you are or how confident you seem to be**. Instead of feeling down because of their taunts, remember that their words say more about their feelings than about you. You're way stronger and more resourceful than you might think! Think about how silly people thought I looked with the tyre. That tyre trained me to pull a sled across Antarctica. **That's not silly, that's awesome!**

If you find your friends or classmates are being unkind, you can always talk to a trusted adult about it. Sometimes you need help helping yourself.

Antarctica training challenge

Here's a fun activity inspired by the training I did for Antarctica. It's a great way to get a taste of what it's like to prepare for a big expedition. Before starting, make sure to have an adult's supervision and check that the item you're going to carry or drag is not too heavy.

What you'll need:

- A sturdy backpack or a lightweight sled (if you have one). If you don't have a sled, you could use something else as a makeshift sled — like a laundry basket, an old suitcase, a pillowcase or a large bag. When you have this item, ask an adult to tie some rope around it and then you can try to drag it.

- Some books or items of a similar weight, like toys or other objects (make sure they're not too heavy). These will represent your supplies for the adventure.

- An outdoor space, which will be your training course.

Let's get ready

Start by packing your backpack or sled with the items you're using as supplies.

Now it's time to create a training regimen, just like I did with my tyre training. Your goal is to simulate the physical preparation for an adventure.

Here's what to do, depending on whether you're using a backpack or a sled:

Option 1 – Carrying challenge: Put your adventure bag on your back. You can adjust the weight by adding or removing items.

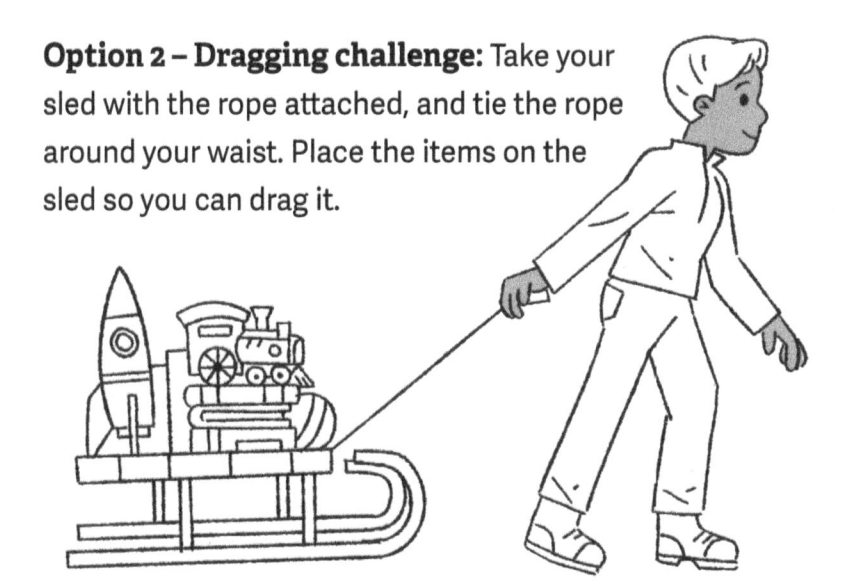

Option 2 – Dragging challenge: Take your sled with the rope attached, and tie the rope around your waist. Place the items on the sled so you can drag it.

Set a timer for your training session. Begin with five minutes of jogging with the backpack on your back or pulling the sled and increase the duration as you get more comfortable.

Bonus activity – Obstacle course: If your outdoor space allows, create an obstacle course with cones and sticks for you to weave around. This will make your training harder, so don't rush in.

Don't forget to record your progress as you go. After each training session, make a note of how you felt. **Did it get easier over time?**

And if you enjoyed the activity, why not share it with your friends and family? Invite them to try it out too. You can even organise a friendly competition to see who can carry or drag the furthest.

Remember, adventure training is not only about building physical strength but also about **developing resilience and determination and having fun.** Enjoy your mini adventure, and who knows, maybe one day you'll embark on a grand expedition of your own!

Believe in yourself

Now, here's a big secret for you young adventurers: you don't need anyone else to tell you how utterly amazing you are. **Inside you, there's a heart brimming with bravery, a mind full of fantastic ideas and the power to make incredible things happen.** I know it might sound easy for me to say, **'Believe in yourself!'** – but even when you're not quite sure, just remember to take it one step at a time. Honestly, that's what I do. Even when self-doubt creeps in, I take it one step at a time.

Explorer's top tip

Whenever you face challenges or doubts, remember this tip from an explorer like me – setbacks are just opportunities to shine brighter. Every time you face a tough situation, you're learning, growing and getting stronger. Keep that in your heart and keep exploring!

Your inner explorer

Deep within you, there's an **explorer eager to uncover the wonders of the world with curiosity and creativity.** Whether you dream of diving into the ocean's depths, reaching for the stars or something entirely new, your dreams are precious and worth chasing.

So whenever you stumble upon doubts or hear someone being unkind about you, be your own biggest cheerleader. Whisper to yourself, **'I can do it!'** Your unique ideas and adventures are what make you wonderfully special, so trust in your talents and have the courage to embark on any adventure, no matter what people say.

Be your own most enthusiastic supporter and you'll achieve wonders beyond your wildest dreams!

CHAPTER FIFTEEN

THE AMAZING NATURE TREASURE HUNT

Now that you have all the skills you need to be a master explorer, it's time to put that knowledge to the test. Are you ready for an exciting adventure that's all about fun, learning and being outdoors? Put on your detective hats, because we're going on a **nature treasure hunt**!

Treasure seekers

In this nature treasure hunt, you'll have to use all your explorer instincts and knowledge to find these items. You'll need to know where to look for them, how to retrieve them, what rules you need to follow along the way and what equipment you might need to bring with you.

Your treasure hunt checklist

Before we dive into our adventure, let's make a checklist of things to find in nature.

📍 **A pine cone:** Spot a pine cone, whether it's on the ground or still hanging from a tree. You can take home fallen pine cones.

📍 **Animal tracks:** Look for footprints or tracks made by animals' or birds' feet. Can you trace or draw them?

📍 **A smooth rock:** Find a rock that feels nice and smooth when you touch it. Put it in your pocket.

📍 **A variety of leaves:** Collect leaves from at least three different trees.

📍 **Wildflowers:** Seek out a beautiful wildflower in bloom and draw a picture of it.

- 📍 **A bird feather:** Keep an eye out for a feather to draw, but remember, never bother a bird!

- 📍 **An insect or a bug:** Spy a tiny creature crawling or flying around. Don't pick it up!

- 📍 **Something red:** Discover something in nature that's the colour red and take a photo of it.

- 📍 **A cloud animal:** Look up at the sky and find a cloud that looks like an animal. Show your adventure buddy.

- 📍 **A nature sound:** Close your eyes, listen carefully and identify a sound from nature around you.

Why not write your own checklist and play this game with your friends? Remember to include something to hear, a colour to find, something to collect and something that makes you look up.

Get exploring!

Grab your checklist, a small bag or basket to hold your treasures and go outside. You can do this treasure hunt in your local park, your garden or even while taking a nature hike. If you're with friends or family, turn it into a friendly competition to see who finds everything first!

Maybe you could use your nature craft skills to create a prize for the winner.

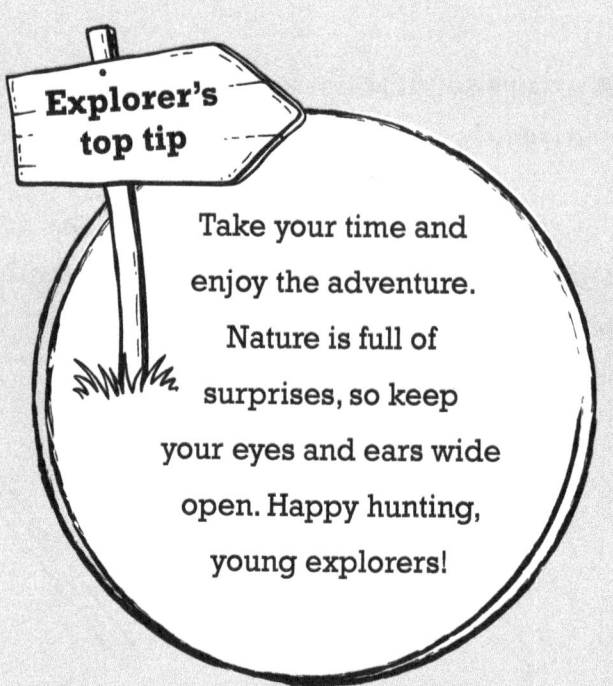

Explorer's top tip

Take your time and enjoy the adventure. Nature is full of surprises, so keep your eyes and ears wide open. Happy hunting, young explorers!

Tricky challenges

Why not make your treasure hunt even more exciting with these extra challenges:

- **Nature art:** Use the leaves and rocks you found to create a beautiful picture.

- **Story time:** Invent a short story about a nature adventure using your discoveries.

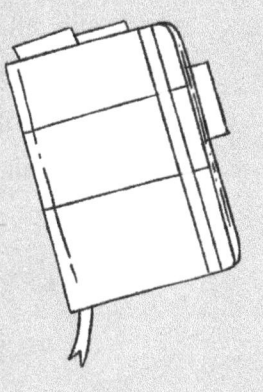

- **Sound map:** Draw a map and mark where you heard each nature sound.

- **Mini research:** Pick one animal you saw and learn five facts about it from a book or online.

Sharing your discoveries

After you've completed your treasure hunt, write about your findings in your journal or tell your friends and family all about them. Describe what you found, where you found it and what you learned about each item. It's a fantastic way to start conversations about nature and all its incredible secrets.

Let yourself go wild

Nature treasure hunts are an exciting way to explore the great outdoors, learn about the environment and have tons of fun. **They encourage curiosity and careful observation, turning you into a true nature detective.** So, young adventurers, go ahead and embark on your very own nature treasure hunt. The treasures of nature are waiting for you to uncover them. Happy hunting!

THE GRAND FINALE

YOUR ADVENTURE AWAITS!

Congratulations, young explorer! You've reached the end. Now all that's left is to get out there and start your adventure. But before you go, I want to leave you with some final words of wisdom – my top tips for discovering adventure and unlocking the outdoors.

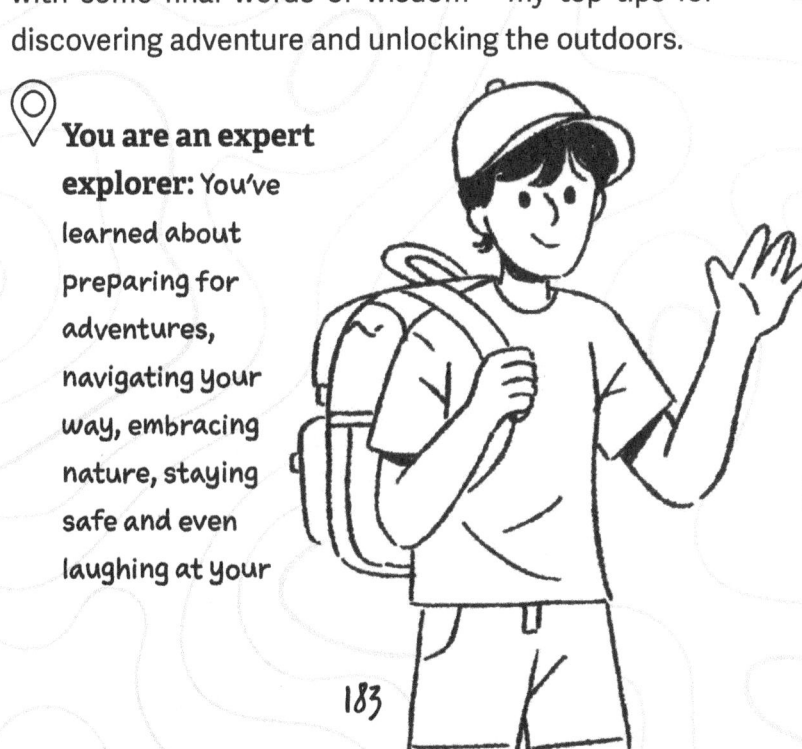

- **You are an expert explorer:** You've learned about preparing for adventures, navigating your way, embracing nature, staying safe and even laughing at your mistakes. Guess what? You're now equipped with the knowledge and mindset of a true expert explorer. Whether you're climbing trees in your local park or dreaming of travelling to distant mountains, you've got the skills to make your journey amazing.

Dream big, start small: Remember, every big adventure starts with a small step. Just like I began with an idea about going to Antarctica, you can start by dreaming big and taking small actions. Whether you're planning a garden camping trip or setting your sights on distant lands, the adventure begins with you.

You are unstoppable: Along your journey, you've discovered just how resilient and brave you are. With determination and a positive outlook, you can overcome anything that comes your way. You've seen how I turned my setbacks into stepping stones in

Antarctica, and you can do the same in your own adventures. Remember, you're not alone on this journey. There are plenty of fellow explorers out there rooting for you.

📍 **Keep exploring, keep learning:** Adventure isn't just about exploring the world around you; it's also about exploring who you are and what you're capable of. Whether you're climbing mountains or trying new hobbies, every experience adds to the incredible story of your life.

📍 **Adventure awaits; go and get it:** As you close this book, remember that every day is a chance for a new adventure. So go on — put on your explorer's hat, grab your curiosity and embark on new expedition. Whether it's in your garden, your neighbourhood or beyond, the world is waiting for you to explore it.

Thank you for joining me on this adventure. Your spirit, enthusiasm and determination inspire me, and I can't wait to see the incredible journeys you'll take. Keep exploring, keep dreaming and keep believing in yourself. Adventure is out there and you're a master explorer, so go wild!

With all my explorer's heart, Preet

Quiz answers

The good explorer's quiz
1: B
2: B
3: C
4: C
5: A

Embrace challenges
1: A
2: A
3: B
4: B
5: B
6: A
7: B
8: B

Can you fix it?

1. Use duct tape if you have it in your backpack. If not, try to tie the ends of the tear together.

2. Find a clean spot with some leaves or grass. Rub your hat to remove the mud and it should be much cleaner.

3. Put your hand in your pocket or tuck it under your arm. Both are simple ways to warm up cold fingers.

4. Use a piece of string or a rubber band as a makeshift shoelace to keep your shoes on your feet.

5. Tie the stick to your backpack with a piece of string or a belt. This makes it easier to carry.

6. Look for small sticks or tape to mend it. If it's beyond repair, try to adapt and use it in a different way.

7. Use a small piece of tape to hold the lens in place, so you can still wear your sunglasses.

8. Use the torch's reflector as a small mirror to catch some light from the moon or stars to see a little better in the dark.

ACKNOWLEDGEMENTS

Firstly, I wanted to acknowledge the wonderful team at Hachette who believed in me.

Helen, for giving me direction and reminding me of my deadlines!

Ben at The Soho Agency, for all of your support, and Aditi, thank you for making my words come to life.

Thank you so much to everyone in the team for helping get this book on to paper. I couldn't have done it without you.

Harpreet Kaur Chandi MBE is a British physiotherapist and British Army medical officer who is the first woman of colour to complete a solo expedition across Antarctica to the South Pole (ending January 2022). In January 2023, she broke the Guinness World Records title for the longest ever solo and unsupported one-way polar ski expedition, travelling 922 miles across Antarctica in 70 days.

IF YOU LIKE THIS BOOK, WHY NOT TRY...